'One daughter. One son. Two d fascinating insight into how gender inequality our society from the earliest years of a child's life.'

– Jo Swinson, Lib Dem MP

'An arresting account of the way casual everyday comments about children reflect and reinforce gender stereotypes. We recommend this book at least once a week – it explains why we campaign.'

– Let Toys Be Toys

of related interest

Are You a Boy or Are You a Girl?
Sarah Savage and Fox Fisher
Illustrated by Fox Fisher
ISBN 978 1 78592 267 1
eISBN 978 1 78450 556 1

Can I tell you about Gender Diversity?
A guide for friends, family and professionals
CJ Atkinson
Illustrated by Olly Pike
ISBN 978 1 78592 105 6
eISBN 978 1 78450 367 3
Part of the Can I tell you about…? series

Straight Expectations
The Story of a Family in Transition
Peggy Cryden, LMFT
ISBN 978 1 78592 748 5
eISBN 978 1 78450 537 0

Who Are You?
The Kid's Guide to Gender Identity
Brook Pessin-Whedbee
Illustrated by Naomi Bardoff
ISBN 978 1 78592 728 7
eISBN 978 1 78450 580 6

THE GENDER AGENDA

A First-Hand Account of How Girls and Boys Are Treated Differently

Ros Ball and James Millar
Foreword by Marianne Grabrucker

Jessica Kingsley *Publishers*
London and Philadelphia

First published in 2017
by Jessica Kingsley Publishers
73 Collier Street
London N1 9BE, UK
and
400 Market Street, Suite 400
Philadelphia, PA 19106, USA

www.jkp.com

Library of Congress Cataloging in Publication Data
A CIP catalog record for this book is available from the Library of Congress

British Library Cataloguing in Publication Data
A CIP catalogue record for this book is available from the British Library

ISBN 978 1 78592 320 3
eISBN 978 1 78450 633 9

Printed and bound in the United States

For our children. Who are ace.

*With thanks to Simon Vaughan
and Anna Auckland.*

CONTENTS

FOREWORD

After giving a lecture to law students at a German university I found myself in a round of students and young lawyers – females and males. They were brilliant young people. Of course I expected sophisticated questions on legal problems, but none came.

Instead, a woman started the discussion with the question, 'Are you Ms..., the author of the book *There's a Good Girl*? You should know that I was raised according to your book. I remember very well that it was always in the kitchen at home and my mother reread it whenever she had time.' A male student related the same tale. His mother kept the book beside her bed. They started a discussion on gender problems instead of legal issues.

I was expecting criticism, but none came, they agreed with my attempt at a gender-neutral upbringing and assured me that they were happy with the way their parents had guided them to be 'different' from stereotyped gender role models. And as a result, as I could see at the event, females and males were equal in numbers and in their professional positions – in their first employment.

Reading Ros's and James's diary it seems to me that ostensibly things have not changed in 30 years, when it comes to the 'blue and pink', the 'tough man and princess' questions. Nevertheless daily life for young women has changed for the better and young men are starting to pay more attention to family and their kids and are emphasising 'the great career' less – as they were still expected to do one generation before. Statistics in Germany substantiate this trend.

A company employing a generative young guy who is becoming a father can't be sure that he won't ask for paternity leave or part-time work. Not so long ago these things were connected only to women of reproductive age and hereby exacerbated disadvantages in employment.

But I am perplexed: on the one hand, comparing both diaries, obviously nothing had changed in turning a child of female sex into a 'good girl' and a child of male sex into a 'real boy'. All these little stories of a child demanding for this or that, just to be like a girl, a boy, a woman, a man…like all the others, left me bewildered and threw me back 30 years.

How should this polarity be dissolved?

I tried to explain in 1984 why children stick to the role model of 'pink' and 'blue' perseveringly, they wish to be like everybody else to become a proper member of society, to be like 'all other adults'.

In the process of a child's growing up we teach them in many other fields to behave in the way life in 'our' society demands: how to wash hands, to use the toilet, to dress, to use a knife and fork, to be polite, to read and write, to study busily to become a successful person in life. Their duty is to focus on copying the adults' behaviour. We thump it into their brain. And why the hell should it be different for gender issues? How to explain the difference to a three-year-old? I think it is not as much how parents individually guide their children, it is more the issue of the overall impression in our society and the behaviour of both genders in practice.

It will be different in future when not only gender-daddy and gender-mummy are different but also all other adults as seen in advertising, on TV, in politics, in movies, toys and in reality in their jobs.

I had the chance to give a lecture to ten-year-olds in primary school on my specific field in law as a judge.

When they had written down their conclusions on what they learned, one girl's result was, 'Originally I planned to become a movie actress, but now I changed my mind definitely, I will become a judge.'

It is time for women to go into politics and well-paid jobs more than ever, with the intention to alter role models. Furthermore, women should be aware in selecting their future job that they will earn enough to support a family – including gender-daddy. By the way, in more and more young couples she is the one who earns more money than he.

It is time for men to stay at home to alter male role models. Females should stay away from the mirror and from domestic chores.

Margaret Mead, the famous American anthropologist in the 1930s, told her daughter, 'If you cannot abide the dust under the bed you will never be successful in your research,'[1] and Christiane Nüßlein-Volhard, a German awarded the Nobel Prize for Biology, said, 'Women should spend less time in front of the mirror but more time with the microscope.'[2]

For now, the show goes on, I am now a grandmother and I still cannot let go of the subject of blue and pink, male and female behaviour with my one-year-old granddaughter.

For example, when she showed an interest in the carabiners I use for rock-climbing her parents suggested that was a dangerous pursuit for a girl – even though one of the carabiners was pink!

At Christmas her mother, my daughter, planned to present her to all family and guests in a light grey Italian fashion cashmere dress with dark grey dots – no pink, of course: the dress was a present from Granny Marianne. But just before the guests arrived her nappy needed to be changed. It was not a textbook change and the dress got pretty wet! In a hurry I found under the Christmas tree a present from some neighbours, parents of a boy baby two months older than she. They gave blue pyjamas as a Christmas gift – which were meant to be for him but were too small. They fitted her perfectly and my grandchild spent Christmas Day dressed in these *blue* boys' pyjamas and, as one auntie pointed out to my pride, she performed not appropriately at all for a young lady at Christmas dinner!

Maybe when I am a great-grandmother we will have another diary to see if there are any further improvements. But even Rome was not built in a day.

Persistence means altering little things steadily. So keep up the good work!

Marianne Grabrucker, author of *There's a Good Girl: Gender Stereotyping in the First Three Years – A Diary* (1981)

PREFACE

Woop woop, it's the gender police. Woop woop, they're everywhere but it's hard to see them. You may even be one of them – but you're such a secret agent even you don't know you are.

We'd always been dimly aware of the gender police, but it was having children that brought the idea into sharp focus. In 2007 our daughter was born, and a frustration with the pink and blue divide erupted in us. When our son was born three years later, it was a second-hand 1980s book from eBay that helped us make sense of that frustration. That book, *There's a Good Girl: Gender Stereotyping in the First Three Years – A Diary* by German lawyer Marianne Grabrucker, had a significant effect on our lives as parents.

The book is based around a simple but brilliant idea: if you start to make a daily note of the way the world 'polices' a child by gender, you have a record of how girls and boys are not born equal. If they do behave differently, this book gave us some answers as to why. Our kids weren't born different, it was the world around them that was treating them differently. The way people spoke to them and the language they used, the toys and clothes they gave them, and the expectations they had of them – they were enforcing certain gender roles, they were policing their behaviour.

When someone experiences problems at work they are often told to keep a diary as a record, possibly to be used as a body of evidence in a tribunal. Grabrucker's diary had the same sort of power. It compiled the everyday complaint or anecdote into a bigger picture, rather than a jumble of frustrated feelings that something is not right. She notes the effect on her daughter of billboards on the street, casual comments from strangers, and the way other children enforce their understanding of their roles as a boy or girl on their peers.

Grabrucker also examined her own behaviour towards her daughter and found that parents are by no means excepted from this issue, much as they might want to think themselves enlightened.

The book inspired us to start keeping our own Twitter diary about our three-year-old girl and our baby boy and how people treated them differently. We hoped things had improved since the 1980s, but we weren't sure how our experience would be different. The first major change was the way we were able to publish our diary on Twitter every day, to connect with people who were similarly interested in this problem, but also to discuss ways of helping us all to break out of these stereotypes. The other difference is that this is written by both mother *and* father and is about stereotypes of both girls *and* boys. Though we come from a firmly feminist position, what we've learned is that things haven't changed enough since Gloria Steinem said, 'Though we've had the courage to raise our daughters more like our sons, we've rarely had the courage to raise our sons more like our daughters.'[3]

The diary is a mish-mash of angry reactions, disappointment with the world and righteous indignation (not always deployed sensibly, but that's the immediacy of social media for you). But it's also peppered with humour, discussion and ways we tried to push against something that we don't agree with.

Off the back of the diary we were asked to write some blogs for the online magazine *Bea* which allowed us to pull together our thoughts on certain topics. And when Marianne Grabrucker was in London as part of her work as an international lawyer we couldn't miss the chance to get together and let people fire some questions at us. That in turn gave birth to a presentation about our experience that we've given at organisations like the BBC and Viacom – the firm that owns Nickelodeon and MTV. When James went part time he published some blogs that were well received. We've pulled these extra resources together in this book too along with crowd-sourced lists of books and films that challenge the orthodoxy and give kids a chance to see strong female and sensitive male characters.

We hope it helps you to think about the ways you were treated as a child, and the way you treat children now. We certainly didn't write it to openly criticise anyone's parenting – more often than not we learned about our own behaviour – our aim was just to expose the thin veneer of equality around us all. It can seem invisible at times, but we hope that if you can see it, you'll want to change it too.

Ros Ball and James Millar, February 2017

THE
DIARY

The diary is reprinted here from our Twitter feed @GenderDiary with some corrections and edits, and swapping text-speak for real words.

10th January 2011

This account is inspired by Marianne Grabrucker's *There's a Good Girl: Gender Stereotyping in the First Three Years – A Diary*. Things happen to our children on a daily basis that make us aware of sex-role conditioning but to which so many people seem oblivious. We'll be tweeting about everyday things that people say and do that seem to confirm gender consciousness to our children.

Taken to the panto by her granny this weekend our daughter and her cousins were buying toys at a stall. Her two older male cousins said, 'Why don't you get this?' and directed her to the pink fluffy tiara. One of her male cousins chose a flashing torch which had pink plastic casing. The woman on the stall said, 'Shall I get you that in blue?'

11th January 2011

Being shown round her new nursery a member of staff said to our daughter, 'This is what we call the boys' corner.' It's a play table for cars.

One of my nephews started school yesterday. His mum couldn't find his hairbrush to comb his messy curly hair. His older brother laughed at him and said he looked 'like a girl'.

12th January 2011

This quote from Marianne Grabrucker sums it up well: 'Children are classified as being typical or untypical of their sex...human behaviour, with varying natural talents and preferences, does not exist.'[4]

At a baby clinic getting our baby boy weighed today. I notice how the health visitors praise heavy boy babies, 'Isn't he a lovely big boy?' Both our children have been at the heavy end of the scale but I haven't heard my girl or other people's being called 'a lovely big girl'. It's possible some people wouldn't like their girl to be called big in size. We refer to girls as big when they are being 'grown up'. I have a friend whose pet name for her son is 'Big boy'. She doesn't call her daughter 'Big girl'.

Evidence-based research shows that of babies rated by their parents at no more than 24 hours old, girls were perceived to have finer features, boys were perceived to be bigger, stronger and better co-ordinated. But there were actually no overall differences between the babies. It's possible boys are handled more roughly from the day they are born for this reason.

13th January 2011

Third day of tweeting was a quiet day. Only thing to report that was odd is daughter saying when the baby gurgles, 'That's like a girl.' When asked what a boy baby sounds like she says a boy cries and that happy noises are 'like a girl'. No idea what this means.

Also want to add a couple of back-dated things. A comment from a shop assistant in a shoe shop when our daughter was two and was climbing around with her nappy showing from under her skirt, 'Don't show everyone that. That's your special secret.' Repeat: two and in nappies.

14th January 2011

Today we had visitors. Our daughter wanted to wear a bridesmaid's dress she had worn for a friend's wedding. She said she wanted to wear her dress because the visitors 'will like me'. She was right I suppose. A girl in a frilly dress gets a lot of 'Don't you look lovely in your pretty dress!', etc. She obviously associates people appreciating her appearance with being liked. There isn't much discussion from visitors about what our boy is wearing or how pretty he looks.

15th January 2011

A friend told me about a little boy she knows who likes dressing up in necklaces, hats and handbags. She isn't very comfortable with this. Although girls' and boys' toys and games are often gender segregated, girls have more freedom to play with so called 'boys' toys'. The friend has a baby boy herself. Like a vast majority of parents of boys, she won't be encouraging dressing up games that are 'for girls'. I wonder what the fear is for the sons who might play dressing up in necklaces. The fact being called a girl is an insult says a lot.

16th January 2011

A little more clarity from the three-year-old on why her baby brother is 'like a girl'. She says it's because 'only girls smile'. Tempted to assume that this might be to do with adverts and general cultural messages about women's appearances. But who knows.

17th January 2011

Just picked up our eldest from nursery. All the boys were sitting at one table with cars and trucks. All the girls on the floor with a game. I have heard the staff reinforce this behaviour before. Some might claim the children's behaviour informs the adult response, but how can you prove which came first? Staff also encouraged our daughter to 'come and play with the girls' on her first day.

20th January 2011

Keeping this diary we've got to be honest about how we might be treating our boy and girl differently as well. Clothes are where we really can't escape social convention without making a big statement. Our boy is in purple today but mostly he's in the standard blue and sludge brown colours. All hand-me-down clothes come ready sorted by gender but it's the one area where very few people dare to tread – putting boys in 'girl colours'. It seems more socially acceptable for girls to wear 'boys' clothes/colours'. Why is it so unacceptable for boys to be like girls at all?

21st January 2011

At the doctors, a friendly old gentleman asks if the baby is a boy. He says how nice it is that we have one of each then tells me, 'It's good because one day he'll be able to do your decorating and she'll be able to cook for you.' I point out that in our house Dad is a good cook and Mum is good at woodwork. He immediately tells me that his son-in-law does the cooking. People so often repeat gender stereotypes despite people in their own experience contradicting them. That's why kids who have stay at home dads will still draw a picture of their mum cooking because that is what they think a 'mum' is.

23rd January 2011

'While a child's sex alone does not determine what is achievable, societies' (or parental) beliefs that girls and boys are innately different can limit their lives' (Dr Pam Lowe, Aston University). That's such a useful quote. It was in a letter to the *Guardian* following an article about couples who pay to choose the sex of their baby.[5] When you think about it, it's clear that wanting a particular gender of child means you already have expectations of their behaviour.

Visiting friends today, a couple of them discussed a friend's baby and how he was 'such a boy' because he went from one thing to the next very quickly. He is six months old. It reminded me how our children's grandmother claimed that one of our nephews was 'being a boy' when he messed around with his pudding, on the same day our daughter had spent all day playing with a toy garage. No one said her behaviour was 'just like a girl'. In fact no one noticed it. The attribution of certain behaviours to the child's gender only seems to apply when it fits the correct stereotype. Our daughter sometimes mucks around with her pudding too, but apparently this can't be attributed to her gender. Pah.

24th January 2011

Recently our daughter turned three and was given a marble run. One of her grandparents said, 'I think your daddy will want to play with that too.' This is an odd thing to say when she knows that marble runs are a particular favourite of Mummy in this family. But the message is made to the kid that anything mechanical is male.

Today, our daughter tells me suddenly, unprompted, about her toy baby, 'My baby is a girl.' I wonder why she suddenly wanted to express this. It makes me notice how important gender is to children from a young age. Picking up daughter from nursery the children crowd round the baby and ask, 'Is it a boy?' I say yes and wonder, now they know this, what difference it makes to them.

25th January 2011

Only been tweeting for two weeks but have been amazed at how often there has been something to tweet about. Almost every day. An obvious one this, but a reminder of the different treatment from day one: a friend who has just had a baby girl is very popular and has a house full of cards. There is only one that isn't pink.

26th January 2011

You could write an essay on gender issues in kids' TV programmes but a couple of things to mention. Today we saw the second of two different programmes that had a plot on the embarrassment of a male character because he is wearing pink. If it's OK for males to be embarrassed of being in any way 'like a girl' in quite benign kids' TV shows then it's very deep in our culture.

We'll also have to do a count of male and female characters. But in a lot of the shows we watch most characters are male, with one female. It's as though male characters can have different personalities but there is only one type of female.

Reading local internet forum for parents, a mum asks for advice on how to get her three-year-old daughter to sleep. No one knows the child personally. Advice is to bribe her, which makes sense. But with sparkly socks, or Disney Princess figures. We're currently bribing our daughter to take unpleasant medicine. The prize on offer? A wind-up torch.

When it comes to sexism there really is no business like the toy business. The Toy Awards last night included categories for boys' toy and girls' toy. That begs so many questions in the first place. Boys' winner was a Nerf gun, girls' winner the Barbie dog swimming pool. Sums it up. Violence for boys, pets and pink for girls. Hard to see how anyone 'wins' at those awards.

27th January 2011

At the doctors, a girl appears from behind us in the waiting room. Our daughter asks, 'Where did she come from?' I say, 'From behind you.' Daughter says, 'No, I mean where is her mummy?' I say, 'Maybe she's here with her daddy?' Daughter is nonplussed. It's not a big surprise that she always expects a child to be with their mother, it is her usual experience of other children I suppose. Although there were actually two fathers with their children in the doctor's waiting room.

We went into the leisure centre later where they sell goggles. She cheerfully told me, 'These ones are for girls and these are for boys.' They were of course pink and blue goggles. I asked her if the blue ones *had* to be for boys and the pink for girls. She said no, so I asked which ones she would wear, she pointed to a purple pair.

28th January 2011

Daughter was given a small LEGO® alien, and it made me consider how we automatically refer to toys as 'he'. Even I couldn't stop myself when I asked, 'What shall we call him? Is he a boy or a girl?' Luckily she wasn't swayed by my language, though, she said, 'Lucy'. Unless a toy has stereotypical female features, or is a doll, people always say 'he'. Babies are usually girls though.

29th January 2011

Kids TV programme on Channel 5 just now called *Play*. It's just a mini-documentary of kids, well, playing. At first all kids play hide and seek but then just the boys are shown playing with huge water pistols which are styled on automatic machine guns.

30th January 2011

Although this diary is about how other people treat our children differently, it's making it clearer that we should look at our own behaviour. Marianne Grabrucker noticed how boys are given free rein to be unruly while girls are more compliant because they are expected to be 'good'. Boys not doing as they are told is more readily accepted because it is expected of them. Can we manage to change this in our own actions?

31st January 2011

Have had two conversations in the last 24 hours with mothers saying how their 2–3-year-old girl wants to 'mother' a smaller child or a doll. Makes me wonder if it's just the girl showing interest in a baby and that's what they label it. Boys are often interested in babies but people don't comment on it much or label it as boys wanting to 'father' the baby.

Falling asleep tonight daughter tells me how something she said, 'Sounds like a boy, but I'm not, I'm a girl.' I ask what a boy sounds like, she makes a sort of grunting noise as though she's lifting something heavy and says, 'That's like a boy.' Then says in a very exaggerated high-pitched voice, 'But I sound like this, because I'm a girl.' Which I've never heard her do before. Presumably children speak at the same pitch until puberty.

Although of course she may have noticed men and women speak at different pitches. But it seems likely that someone has been pointing out gender differences at nursery today. A boy? She fell asleep before I could ask.

3rd February 2011

Air freshener advert on TV today, daughter says the green can must be for boys, pink one for girls. This is going to be harder than I thought! And I, her dad, was wearing a pink shirt at the time!

Post-match pints with some fellow dads last night. One expresses dismay that he's found recently that he's started 'throwing like a girl'. He, like me, has one daughter and one son. I pointed out to him that language will limit his daughter's ambitions and expectations.

Talking to a father who stayed at home with his baby while his partner went back to work, he said mothers at baby groups were hostile to him. Wonder if other male carers find similar issues?

Our child minder was telling me earlier that (in her long experience) boys take longer to pick up things like putting on shoes and eating with cutlery. But she said she believed it's because parents and carers are more likely to do these things for boys. She said she was also guilty of this despite being aware of it. Is this due to historic cultural roles where women waited on men? Regardless of its origin it's surely a bad thing for boys to be diverted from learning to do things for themselves.

4th February 2011

The purple and grey striped jumper our baby boy is wearing under his dungarees is actually a long jumper-dress but you wouldn't know it. When I was changing him and two mothers saw that it was a dress I was surprised how shocked and disapproving they were. At three-and-a-half months old I don't think he's all that bothered, but their reactions would give an older child a lot to think about. Girls wear trousers without any worries about their sexual identity, are boys so much more fragile? What are these mothers afraid of?

8th February 2011

A trip to the hairdresser for Mum and daughter. Every hairdresser we've ever been to has told her that she 'will look like a princess'. Today while discussing sitting still the hairdresser said, 'You can tell Daddy when he comes home from work that Mummy sat very still.' Actually Daddy was at home looking after the baby, but neither her nor me told the hairdresser this, we just smiled. We should have done.

11th February 2011

A couple of things today. Daughter played at a friend's house and on the way told me, '[My friend] is a *boy* who is nice you know. He doesn't hit his mummy.' It was interesting that her language suggested it was unusual for a boy to be 'nice'. She's right, though, of the boys we know he is definitely the most mild mannered. They had a lovely morning playing together. They played dressing up. He had a hat and said he was a doctor, she had a cape and said she was a princess. Only on Tuesday at the hairdressers was it confirmed to her that being a princess was something she should want to be. Adults have spoken to her about being a princess many more times in her life than being a doctor. I wonder what her male friend's choice of dressing up character is influenced by. I'll take note when our boy is old enough to dress up. But I'm guessing no one will have told him he looks like a princess on a regular basis.

12th February 2011

Thoughts about not buying children toys in stereotypical colours/styles? Our daughter wanted a bike for Christmas and we looked hard for a gender-neutral one but she requested it have handlebar streamers and a baby seat on the back. Obviously only the 'girl' bikes had these accessories. We did get her one. It's hard to withhold things when she is too young to understand your ideology. Seeing the gendered bikes in the park today makes me wish we hadn't.

Should we state whether it's Dad or Mum tweeting? Or is that defeating the purpose somewhat? I mean should we specify who is authoring each tweet? I'm inclined not to.

Some classic stuff from a dads and kids meet-up this afternoon. Four-year-old girl showing off ballet moves she learned at class this morning. Two-year-old brother copies by lifting leg up and a dad says, 'Oh he's like Jean Claude Van Damme.' Wow.

Two girls there go off to play with a doll's house and a dad points to this as 'typical' of girls, evidence of innate differences. Girls return and start playing with toy tool kit, one drilling, one hammering a door. Same dad barely registers that 'untypical' behaviour. The doll's house was upstairs, everyone else is downstairs. Are the girls' actions indicative of confidence to play away from parents/adults? Plus my girl only knew of the doll's house because when we arrived the three-year-old boy of the host took her off to play with it. No one commented until the two girls were playing with the doll's house.

Our four-year-old girl was a bit shy and clingy when first arrived. It was blamed on the fact all the toys of the three-year-old host are 'boys' toys'. But it didn't faze our daughter. She was happily playing with trucks, fire engines, etc. and no one comments. Yet if what is said about 'boys' toys' is true then her behaviour is unusual and therefore surely more worthy of comment? Gender attitudes are self-reinforcing.

16th February 2011

Some thought-provoking stuff this week that is not black and white. Marianne Grabrucker wrote about boys dominating play so girls had to adapt their behaviour. Yesterday our daughter played with a boy who is the stereotype of a 'boys' boy'. As with every time they play he wants whatever the other child has, not to play with it though, but in order to have ownership of it and to be the one in charge. I've seen girls be possessive of toys too, though, and they will also take something just to have ownership. But it never escalates to the same level as with this boy. We end up taking the toy away from them both, so the girl loses out even though she has done nothing. Grabrucker argues that the girl has to adapt to the boy's behaviour which sets them up for the patriarchal world. I think children of both genders would behave like this if they could. I can only conclude boys do it more because they are allowed to do so.

19th February 2011

A three-year-old's birthday party today and there were a lot of things we could tweet about, but one thing struck me (Mum) most; daughter had mentioned wearing a dress to the party but had forgotten by the time we left so I didn't remind her. When we arrived the birthday girl and a friend were in party dresses. I immediately worried that my girl would feel left out, but this was my worry not hers. I remembered a birthday party I had been to as a child where I didn't know most of the children and they had bullied me because I wore boyish clothes. I suppose this experience pushed me into conforming more in what I wore. I wanted to fit in. Will she? For the record the boys were wearing their everyday clothes just like my daughter. When she was a bridesmaid she learned, and said, people 'like me' in a pretty dress. She noticed they give her special attention for it. I'd rather she got a compliment for something she did or said, but I expect she'll remember to put on a dress next time. I won't stop her if she wants to.

24th February 2011

At a playground today daughter played with a boy who was dressed in beige and brown and was very forthright. If they were on a play boat he said, 'I'm the captain,' or if I tried to help he said, 'I can do that,' repeatedly. When he left daughter said, 'There she goes.' I asked why she thought he was a girl. She said, 'She's got long hair.' Interesting that for a three-year-old long hair was the most important way to define gender despite other signifiers. He had a ponytail. Though I suppose actually I don't know for sure whether she/he was a boy or a girl.

6th March 2011

So I should start by saying that the National Railway Museum is really great and we had a great time there, however the museum had a kids' science presentation about Newton's Laws – the way forces make trains move. The show needed audience volunteers. Every single child called up as a volunteer was a boy until they did an experiment with a Barbie doll. The presenter asked if there were any Barbie fans who wanted to help. A whole pack of Cubs had their hands in the air but finally a girl volunteer was picked. Poor Barbie got fired out of a cannon and her legs broke off, much to the amusement of the audience. An earlier experiment used two toy elephants to demonstrate how weight affects force, one was in pink and one in blue. The blue elephant had eaten a full English breakfast and was heavy. The pink elephant had had a glass of water and was on a diet. Science is so often gender segregated and this was no exception.

11th March 2011

Yesterday a friend came to play with her three-year-old boy and one-year-old girl. I asked what toys they would like me to get out. I suggested DUPLO®, musical instruments, cars or dressing up. My friend said she was sure her boy would want to play with the cars. He didn't seem more interested in them than any other toys to me. Later she asked her girl, 'Wouldn't you like to try on the fairy wings?' She said no. I often see blatant directing of children into gendered play like this, yet parents don't notice their own influence. Isn't it obvious?!

15th March 2011

A friend said her three-year-old boy asked her, 'What do you call a girl's willie?' and she didn't know what to say. She asked me what we call it. I said when our daughter was a baby we called her genitals her 'fandango' but didn't often say that any more. We agreed it was a shame that names for girls' genitals are so overlooked. Marianne Grabrucker gave her daughter's genitals the name Mary-Ann and used the name frequently. Boys' genitals are obviously more prominent and are easily talked about, but why should it be that we don't talk about girls' genitals?

19th March 2011

What I've noticed most of all by keeping this diary is the acceptance of raising boys to shun anything with female connotations. So where girls wear clothes, or read books, or watch films about both genders, the same is not true of boys. And we accept this. There has to be a point where we ask what messages it sends to boys to be brought up to always reject the female realm.

20th March 2011

Talking to a friend whose son is four in a few weeks. She's talking about the difficulty of making him the dinosaur birthday cake he wants. No such problems with her seven-month-old daughter, she's already got a fairy princess castle recipe lined up.

25th March 2011

The @GenderDiary family is at Peppa Pig World (sigh). I am pleased to say it is measuring up very well so far in the gender-neutral stakes. But even though the main character is Peppa, all the 'boys' clothes' have her brother George on. Boys can't be seen wearing the female character.

27th March 2011

On train to the TUC march yesterday a granny was telling another woman that her granddaughter is excited about a new baby. Granny said, 'If it's a boy you can play football with him.' The friend interjects to say she could play football with a girl, 'It could turn out to be a tomboy.' Close. Actually she could play football with a girl because girls can like football on their own terms!

29th March 2011

In M&S Bromley this afternoon with the two kids. Shop assistant says to me, 'You babysitting this afternoon?' I said nothing. I should've said, 'NO, I'm just a man in a shop with his two children!' Where does one begin??

30th March 2011

Visiting a friend at the weekend who has a one-year-old son. He's walking. She reminds me 'boys mobilise, girls socialise'. This is a mantra I've often shared, I think it's true to some extent, BUT not because of inherent differences, it's because sexes are treated differently from birth. She says she can only speak from experience with her son, that's her scientific experiment. I point out that's not science. If it was how science works I'd look at my children and conclude all boys have blue eyes, all girls have brown eyes! Today's @GenderDiary lesson must surely be to tell people at every opportunity to see the difference between anecdote and evidence.

2nd April 2011

Daughter is at an age when we're thinking about first trip to cinema. Easter releases for kids seem to be *Rio*, *Hop* or *Turtle Story*. All got male lead characters. Not a problem but I say we should have a rule that every second film we see with kids must have a female lead. Trouble is will we ever go to the cinema again?!

6th April 2011

Get ready for a gender tweetathon. Got lots saved up. Hopefully the baby will stay asleep.

First up, an anecdote about a six-year-old who has always been indulged in the fetishism of pink/princesses/Barbies. She has black hair but whenever she draws a picture of herself she draws blonde hair and blue eyes. When asked why, she says that that's what she wants to look like and doesn't want to look like herself. Gulp.

On the way to a pre-school fair this weekend our daughter asked if there would be face painting and could she be a pirate? On the way in we pass two girls with pink butterflies on their faces. Several people in our party tell them how nice they look. We sit down to get her face painted and the painter asks, 'What do you want and what's your favourite colour?' I was gobsmacked, she asked for a pink butterfly. She had only told me earlier her favourite colour was red. The face painter whispered to me she was bored of pink and was running out.

Another anecdote about a two-year-old who is a regular mountain goat, always climbing everything. She was climbing the gate outside her pre-school as she does every day. Her grandparent tried to take her down thinking it unsafe. She protested and the grandparent said, 'Fine, you be a tomboy.' The words were not meant as a criticism but the implication is that a typical girl child wouldn't climb or be interested in it.

My daughter and her cousins were playing dressing up, she had put on fairy wings but was bored of them and asked for something else. We offered her a devil, a witch and a police helmet. She says, 'No! I want something PRETTY!' This feminist tried not to look horrified! Don't be too harsh on me for that last comment, Twitter!

Not many mentions for our baby boy at the moment, although I notice people tell me how strong/big he is more often than I remember with my daughter. Possibly I just notice it more, or possibly people say it more often. (Possibly he's bigger and stronger…)

How could I forget this one: I'm talking with my nephew about something that is broken, he says, 'You need your daddy to fix it for you.' I ask why, he says because his daddy fixes things. I ask if Mummy could fix things. 'No, only daddies fix things.' I ask why he thinks that. He says, 'Because I've never seen Mummy fix anything.' I remind him how I (his aunt) fixed his DVD player.

7th April 2011

Talking to another dad after football about primary schools. His son starts in September, our daughter will start next year. He says he's not concerned about which school his baby daughter will go to because girls have a different way of learning. His son however needs more structure because he's a boy. His daughter is six months, how can he know what sort of education will suit her? Both children being brought up in the same house by the same parents, yet he's convinced gender will determine how they learn from day one at school.

8th April 2011

The @GenderDiary family are off to Germany, home of Marianne Grabrucker, for a week. We'll report back on what's changed in the last 30 years.

18th April 2011

Most interesting thing happened on Sunday. Both of us were looking for books to read at bedtime with our daughter. She found a bookmark with a cartoon of a girl with bunches on it. She said it was for her, but it couldn't be for Daddy. We asked why. She said it could be for Mummy because it was a girl. When pressed she explained that because it looked like her then it was 'for' her. It seemed clear how clearly she sees representations of girls as meaning something is 'for' her, or that she belongs in that sphere.

So, here's a list of things the children's grandmother told me were due to being a boy this week: concentrating very hard on the TV, having a large appetite as a baby, not doing things for themselves like getting dressed. Describes my daughter to a tee.

@GenderDiary Dad was taking out his contact lenses when one of the children we were on holiday with said contact lenses were only for girls. In his experience only his mother wears contact lenses and he had obviously put this down to her gender. He is six and it's interesting how early kids will attribute arbitrary things to gender rather than another factor like having blue eyes or being a doctor, both of which are attributes of his mother. We told him men wore contacts too but he didn't seem very convinced.

20th April 2011

Here's a marvellous quote for you from Cordelia Fine's *Delusions of Gender*, 'Cultural realities and beliefs about females and males represented in existing inequalities; in commercials; in conversations; in the minds, expectations or behaviour of others; or primed in our own minds by the environment – alter our self-perception, interests and behaviour.'[6]

Ditto this quote by sociologists Celia Ridgeway and Shelley Correll, 'Cultural beliefs about gender act like a weight on the scale that modestly but systematically differentiates the behaviour and evaluations of otherwise similar men and women.'[7]

We were away last week with relatives who have a six-year-old boy and a four-year-old girl. While I was sat breastfeeding, the girl came over to me and asked what I was doing and then we chatted about various things. Both her mother and father separately asked me if she had come to talk to me about babies because she was so into them. I told them it didn't seem that way to me. Meanwhile her brother had requested to hold and cuddle the baby on three or four occasions and for quite some time. His sister never did this. No one commented on his interest at all.

Incidentally at the airport in Munich two separate boys around the age of two or three took particular interest in our baby and were encouraged to do so by their parents, which was nice to see.

27th April 2011

The kids' grandmother was telling me how she had been trying to get her son-in-law to fix her grandson's bike tyre so they could go out. I asked why she or my sister thought they couldn't do it. She looked flummoxed and agreed they probably could.

Being able to speak very little German meant we didn't have many lengthy chats about gender while we were away. But I noticed something interesting on the plane. A flight attendant asked, 'How old is she?' referring to our boy who was wearing gender-neutral clothes. It occurred to me that they would have similar conversations very frequently and be well versed in not saying the wrong thing. I wondered if they think that a parent with a girl baby would be more offended at the child being called a boy than vice versa.

Saw our child minder who will be looking after our baby boy later in the year. She was tipping him upside down and saying, 'Ah yes you like things a bit rough. Yes, boys do.' She did then temper it by saying that his sister was like that too. I think physical treatment of boys is subtly different in so many ways.

I've really been noticing how female leads in children's books – fairy tales most often, but other genres too – are referred to as beautiful. This is often the only description of them and is always seen as a virtue and something relevant. Even female characters that are animals are described this way. So Perdita in *101 Dalmatians* is introduced as a beautiful dog. I often leave out these words when reading.

Would be good to see the methodology for this research from the Geena Davis Research Institute – 'They found that the more hours of television a girl watches, the fewer options she believes she has in life, and the more hours a boy watches, the more sexist his views become.'[8] Yikes.

28th April 2011

Delusions of Gender by Cordelia Fine really is bloody fantastic. @GenderDiary would like to buy the whole world a copy. The piece I was just reading that explains how girls' ability in maths depends on which country they are from is fascinating. 'Innate' and 'hardwired' are such overused and misunderstood words.

29th April 2011

Following on from last night's maths tweet. The only thing I've heard Kate Middleton say recently while doing a meet and greet with students:

Kate: What are you studying?

Student: Maths.

Kate: Oh gosh, really?!

Jessica Smith's review of *Delusions of Gender* for the feminist blog, The F-Word[9] makes reference to something I've been trying to do recently. Refer to 'children' rather than 'boys and girls'.

Bank holidays + family = Gender Diary material.

I came in at the end of a conversation between grandparent and my daughter. Grandmother: 'You need your daddy to build the train,' referring to some DUPLO®. I say, 'Why does she need Daddy?!' Grandmother claims that he had made the train really quickly once before and then protested that she is told off by me too often. But honestly, how hard is it to build a train with DUPLO?! It's insulting to three generations of females in the room to suggest we need a man, who's not here (he's working), to stick toy bricks together for us.

Later we went for a walk in the woods with my sister, brother-in-law and three children. It reminded me of an entry in Marianne Grabrucker's diary where she describes little girls pushing toy prams being unable to run and play freely while so tied down. I noticed how myself and my sister were pushing buggies while the kids and my brother-in-law mucked about and he showed them interesting things. I consciously tried to leave the buggy sometimes and get involved because otherwise I felt like we were behaving just like in Marianne's diary from over 30 years ago.

1st May 2011

A Cordelia Fine quote on pink and blue for you, 'So thoroughly have these preferences become ingrained that psychologists and journalists now speculate on the genetic and evolutionary origins of gendered colour preferences that are little more than fifty years old.'[10]

2nd May 2011

I saw a t-shirt in a clothes shop with the slogan 'Daddy's Girl', but I'm guessing they don't make the equivalent 'Mummy's Boy' t-shirt for boys.

Interestingly there are lots more colours for boys' clothes in the shops. Purple, pink and yellow are new and very welcome, however they often come with a signifier to remind us this is a boy.

3rd May 2011

Another example of how gender seems so important that kids attach a relevance to it that doesn't exist. Daughter said, 'Mummies don't go to the hairdressers with children. Only daddies go with children and mummies stay at home to look after the baby.' Oddly her mum has taken her the last two times, but before that it was usually Dad.

We've tweeted before about how kids assume something is only for one gender because in their house someone takes that role. But I think it highlights the way kids use gender as the thing to differentiate rather than, say, blue eyes. Our language and behaviours attach importance to the difference between male and female, so kids do as well.

4th May 2011

Incidentally, a way that we've treated the kids differently is that our boy has had books like *I Love Kittens* from the library which we wouldn't have picked for our girl. It's to try to counter-balance all the gender stereotypical stuff they'll get outside the home so it's justified. Gender-neutral parenting is, of course, an impossibility.

Also, I tried to change one of the animals in a Dr Seuss book to 'she' last night. Our daughter corrected me. I asked why it wasn't a she, she said she just knew it wasn't. To be fair she's read it quite a few times before. There are very few female characters in Dr Seuss.

6th May 2011

An update on what is turning out to be kid's fashion week on @GenderDiary. My nine-year-old nephew just triumphantly told me about his new trainers. 'What colour do you think my laces are?' he asked. I said I had no idea. 'Pink!' he beamed. So pink *is* in fashion for boys. I should mention that this nephew has rarely been seen in anything other than navy blue and sludge brown before. Laces are a good start.

Meanwhile our three-year-old isn't down with the nuances of fashion. She told me earlier, 'Remember how I said blue swimming goggles are for boys and pink for girls? Well that's because girls are pink and boys are blue.' I asked what she meant literally, saying, 'But you're not pink.' She looked down at her clothes and repeated it. I asked if she meant clothes and she said yes. I said that boys don't *have* to wear blue and girls pink. She insisted they do (even though she was wearing blue). I insisted they didn't, she said they did. Etc., etc.

9th May 2011

We were about to go out in the children's grandmother's car this weekend when she realised her tyre was low. She explained this to our daughter, saying, 'We'll have to go in Daddy's... [Pause for though]...AND Mummy's car.' If you persist it seems others change their thinking too.

Dentist visit for the family today. They usually give stickers to reward kids. Disney Princess ones were promised and

@GenderDiary Dad pointed out that we wouldn't be that thrilled about it. The female dentist told us her male nurse only got those ones out for girls and had Rupert Bear ones for boys. The dentist said even if he offers both he holds the gender-specific one further forward. Our daughter was eventually given one of each. Again, we hope our comments might have made them think about their assumptions.

While turning on the TV for our daughter the previous channel comes up. It's the news channel playing a story about Osama Bin Laden. She says, 'I don't like mens (sic!), I like ladies.' I ask what she means and she just repeats it even when I remind her that Daddy is a man. She briefly says she doesn't like men's voices but then reverts to saying she doesn't like 'mens'. It makes me feel a bit sad.

12th May 2011

Stuck in watching TV with a kid covered in chickenpox. Feeling furious at the lack of female characters we're seeing and about their names: Petal, Precious, Sweetie, etc. It's as though the television is trying to wind me up. #angermanagementFAIL

13th May 2011

It's not surprising kids think all gender-neutral animals are male. Show me an adult who doesn't use 'he' as a default and I'd be shocked.

16th May 2011

A lesson learned about calling things by their correct name: as we mentioned once about naming genitals, we've been known to call a vagina a fandango. Who would have thought that word would ever appear in a different context in a kids'

TV programme? But today a puppet vegetable fennel was doing the tango and they called it 'the fandango'. Cue hilarious confusion. We should have just used the word vagina.

20th May 2011

A visit to the Natural History Museum inevitably ends in the gift shop. They have a toy pack that contains a diver and plastic sea animals, and a pack with plastic bones and a dinosaur hunter. Both diver and dinosaur hunter are male. Why? It's even more nutty when on other side of the shop wall is an exhibit about Mary Anning, described as the 'greatest fossil hunter ever known' by the Natural History Museum.

Daughter yesterday says, 'When I grow up I'm going to be a princess AND a pirate.' Is it a sign we're succeeding in balance? Or failing because we can't stop the all-pervasive princess culture?

24th May 2011

A trip to second-rate animal park Eagle Heights at the weekend and there were lots of Cub Scout groups there. The Cubs were all boys, the leaders all middle-aged/elderly women. What are the implications for boys' role models? When I was a Cub, leaders were a range of ages and gender. Are men now afraid of nonce jokes? And boys get the message that volunteering-leadership is for women? Will they then ask why leaders in national life are not women?

25th May 2011

Just remembered a conversation with a colleague the other day. Small talk included him telling me how his teenage boys don't want to wear high visibility jackets when cycling because, 'They'll look like girls.' It's a well-accepted insult, isn't it? #bah

26th May 2011

On the swings with the kids and two girls about 14 are swinging next to us. A girl of about nine starts climbing the metal frame of the swing and, because she's wearing her school skirt, we all see her pants as she crouches on the bar. One of the girls says, 'That's a bit expla…expli…what's it called?' They eventually agree the word they are looking for is 'explicit'. They laugh like drains for quite a while. The nine-year-old leaves quickly. Our daughter watches all this with wide-eyed interest but says nothing.

27th May 2011

We were interviewed by Emily Craig (@emilyjoanhc) this week for a radio documentary she's making about gender and education. Sure it will be marvellous! The documentary considers the Swedish approach to gender in pre-school.

28th May 2011

We love them dearly but the kids' grandparents provide valuable fodder for this diary. Arriving after they are in bed, their grandmother sees the newly acquired PLAYMOBIL® castle/fort our daughter has been given. She says, 'A fort? I won't know how to play with her with that.' 'Why?' I ask. 'I just wouldn't know what to do. It makes me think of fighting.' I say it's just like other imaginary play – a building with people in it. A doll's house for example.

1st June 2011

Yikes. We've just been followed by @BabyGenderPlan 'Plan Your Baby's Gender'. Not planning to click on that link.

Forgive me if I'm wrong but it's legal in parts of the US, no? I'll go and google it. By which I mean being able to choose the sex. There was a piece in the *Guardian* last year about people in this country travelling abroad so they could choose.[11]

There was a great letter in the paper the following week which we still have stuck on our wall. I've quoted it before but will again. (*See 26th June.*)

7th June 2011

Here's an interesting one. A friend's cat gets stuck in a neighbour's shed while they are on holiday. I'm busy talking about the cat on the phone. That cat's name is Sugar and he's male. Our daughter says, 'That's a girl's name.' I ask her to explain why she thinks that is associated with the female and therefore not appropriate for the male. I assume this but she couldn't explain herself enough to be sure.

9th June 2011

I was at parliament this week for Jean Kilbourne speaking to an all-party group on body image, organised by Jo Swinson MP. Jean Kilbourne was a pioneer on how adverts affect body image, she invented the discipline. And she is really nice. Look up her film *Killing Us Softly* on YouTube. Brilliant, funny and incisive. But I think Jean Kilbourne missed a trick in considering not just kids' ads more fully but the extent that kids are gendered before they even see their first ad. Girlguiding offered an interesting point. Girls' role models are Katie Price/Perry, etc., but the values they want are courage and to triumph over adversity.

12th June 2011

Went for coffee with a friend, his son (four) and my daughter. The kids have cookies and crumbs are everywhere, but he only comments on his lad making a mess as a 'typical boy'.

15th June 2011

I find the 'pink' thing is like a creeping contagion. On Monday our daughter wanted to choose her clothes for nursery, 'I want pink leggings because Hannah at nursery's favourite colour is pink.'

Then at a friend's house playing with a girl and a boy of a similar age. The other children fight over who gets a pink cup and plate for their tea. Our daughter then says she wants pink too. Which never happens at home.

25th June 2011

The pink creep continues for our daughter. She was choosing a temporary tattoo from a sheet. They were all butterflies in different colours. She said, 'I want the pink one, because it's the pretty one.' The butterflies are all the same shape so it must be colour that signifies prettiness to her. So the colour alone is now shorthand for it. Pink is no longer just a colour, it is loaded with meaning.

26th June 2011

I said I'd post the ace reply to the article on baby sex selection from the *Guardian* letters page ages ago (*1st June*). Coming next:

> Your article on sex selection matches my own studies in the area to some extent. However, you overlooked the most important element. People want to choose a child's sex

because they believe that sex will determine certain gendered qualities within an imagined child. This can range from boys carrying on the family line to the fetishism of pink princesses in girls. Having set this course for an unborn child, this influences families' understanding and potential treatment of the child, impacting on the child's life chances. While a child's sex alone does not determine what is achievable, societies' (or parental) beliefs that boys and girls are innately different can limit their lives. (Dr Pam Lowe, senior lecturer in sociology, Aston University)[12]

How great is that? It's stuck up in our toilet so most people who visit our house read it. Sneaky, eh? She sums up what we feel very well.

27th June 2011

So, our daughter's favourite film is the old Disney animation *Robin Hood*. When learning this, at least three people have mentioned that she'd make a great Maid Marion or something similar about Maid Marion. She has always identified with Robin Hood – but people want to apply a rule that she must identify with a character of the same gender. It's the same issue we've seen before about gender being taken note of and considered more important than any other aspect of a person's character.

One about the baby as well today. The old classic, 'He's such a boy!' The comment came just from looking at him, he wasn't doing anything. I was holding him. Someone else asked, 'How old is she?' about five minutes later.

28th June 2011

At a magic show. The magician asks the kids in the audience their names. One girl is shy, so he says, 'Girls are often a bit more embarrassed.' He ignores my daughter desperately trying to get his attention so she'll be asked! Later in the show our daughter gets to go on stage to help with a trick. A little boy also goes up. The magician banters with them, only my daughter is asked, 'Are you married?' Mum and Dad aren't married never mind the three-year-old daughter. When the little boy is asked he says he wants to be a shopkeeper when he grows up. My girl says she wants to be a pirate.

29th June 2011

Been thinking about this Lisa Bloom piece 'How to talk to little girls',[13] without the words 'Hello, what a pretty DRESS!' and knowing we also need to learn how to talk to boys. Research shows we talk to them much less.

8th July 2011

Things that are due to being a boy No.1743: Being hot. Visitor today: 'I think that's a boy thing because [name of other boy] is always hot.'

9th July 2011

Bought a fleece for son. It's mainly blue with pink stripes but was in the girls section. Who decides how much pink makes an item female?

Also the first time he wore it was the first time in eight months he's been mistaken for a girl.

To the cinema last week with some trepidation for *Tinkerbell and the Great Fairy Rescue*. Part of my rule that every second film we see has a female lead. The worry is that even female-led films will feature nothing but princesses, fairies, etc. Tinkerbell was OK though, she's practical, fixes and makes things.

11th July 2011

Tonight our daughter was cutting up an old card with pictures of cakes on it, 'The beautiful cakes are the girls' cakes, and the not good ones are boys.' I say boys are beautiful too. She says no. I tell her that means she's saying her dad and brother aren't beautiful. She says that's right. Today is a nursery day. Things like this often get said after being at nursery.

13th July 2011

Just remembered a they're-like-that-because-they're-a-boy/girl thing from the weekend. A mum tells me her baby girl 'is feisty because she's a girl'. Although it's nice to hear a more unusual generalisation about girls (instead of them being 'good' compared to boys), it is nonetheless something being applied as being caused by gender, when it's really just down to personality.

14th July 2011

Something I've noticed recently is how many women put themselves down in front of their kids. It's not surprising they do it with the pressures that advertising and the media place on women and their appearance. But you can see how children will listen and be affected.

Please tell me the new Smurf film doesn't have only one female Smurf. Please no.

16th July 2011

Went to a primary school fair today. The 'Test your strength' stall had prizes of toy guns, swords and bows & arrows. There were boys everywhere with weapons. One was heard to say, 'Anyone who doesn't want to be friends gets shot!' I didn't see any girls with the prizes.

22nd July 2011

Spent afternoon at daughter's nursery 'graduation' for those leaving to go to school. Entertainment included balloon animals and face painting. Face painting was a very strict gender split of pink butterflies or cats for girls and tigers for boys. Reactions from adults for girls, 'Don't you look pretty/beautiful.' For boys, less comment, but usually, 'Don't you look scary.' Kids were aged 3–4 and were asked by the painter what they wanted. Shows how fixed gender conformity is by this age. Daughter chose a tiger when she was two but since being three has always asked for a pink butterfly. The painter asks each child their favourite colour too. She says pink, although doesn't say this at home.

25th July 2011

Today I've been noticing in my own thoughts how strong the impulse is to look at my baby boy's behaviour and compare it to his sister's; how I could think, while reading a book with him for example, 'He's a boy, he'd rather be active,' even though his sister may have acted in a similar way. But would some people then make less of an effort to continue with the book with a boy? This would allow boys more opportunity to be active and girls to be more static, bookish and to be talked to. Does this allow boys more 'freedom', but at the expense of communication skills?

28th July 2011

Just saw a poster for the Smurf movie. I was gobsmacked. Yes there is still just one female. Because being female is a character trait y'know. Going to have to look up the plot of the current Smurf film now. Ug.

Smurf plot: They are in New York and have to get home. Jeez, no one has EVER thought of that idea before. I'm so sorry I had to share that. No mention of the ratio of male to female Smurfs in the coming film. Posters suggest it's one Smurfette.

Incidentally I see Studio Ghibli's new film of the Borrowers is out soon, with title changed to the name of the female lead Arrietty. Good.

29th July 2011

Daughter settled no bother at all when she first went to the child minder. Fair to say our son is less keen, but still only his first week. I was telling someone that it had been a little difficult and she says, 'Well he's a boy.' What does that even mean?? #blamegenderforeverything

30th July 2011

Daughter is talking in the park. She says to me, 'There's a mummy squirrel. The daddy squirrel is out at work.' I say, 'That squirrel is looking for food, that's squirrel work! Just like your mummy goes to work.'

Maternity leave only being economically viable for the woman in our house has given our daughter access to a classic standard view of men going to work while women stay at home. Maternity leave is over now, so it will be interesting to see how fixed her assumptions are.

6th August 2011

Earlier I caught myself thinking, 'When our daughter's friend comes to play he'll really enjoy playing with her PLAYMOBIL® castle.' I then remembered in our last two visits to his house his mother had got out a Fisher Price doll's house specifically for our daughter. I disregarded it at the time as me just being very 'gender-sensitive', after all, it's a toy belonging to a boy.

But now I see she probably had the same train of thought as me, which is basically directing children to toys based on their gender. I'll ask her next time.

7th August 2011

We've been watching #CBeebies for 45 mins and only heard one female character speak. Do me a favour world.

12th August 2011

Today our daughter says, 'Girls wear bows in their hair. Boys can't. If a boy wore a bow I'd tell him I wouldn't be his friend any more.' Cue long conversation about all the problems with those statements. It's amazing what has been picked up by the age of three-and-a-half.

15th August 2011

A wedding this weekend. Interesting for kids to hear in the speeches the many references to the bride's appearance but never to the groom's. To be fair to them, they walked into the church together and both made speeches. Quite modern!

Books come up frequently in the diary gender divide. I saw Anne Frank's *The Diary of a Young Girl* in the library today with a sticker on that says, 'Something for the girls'. The sticker may as well say, 'BOYS! Despite the lessons for all of humankind in this book, it is about a GIRL and therefore not for you!'

17th August 2011

Amazing. Just heard a UK survey shows, on average, boys get 32p more pocket money than girls. We start the gender pay gap in the home! Awful. We keep this diary purely to record the way kids experience the world differently because of their gender, because so many people believe they don't.

19th August 2011

Diet book aimed at 6–12-year-old girls![14]

22nd August 2011

I am dressing our baby boy and putting him in his pink polo shirt (sold as a boy's shirt). Discussion with six-year-old nephew as follows:

Six-year-old: Why are you doing that?

Me: I'm getting him dressed.

Six-year-old: But why are you dressing him in that?

Me: These are his clothes.

Six-year-old: But it's pink.

Me: Yes, it's a colour. I'm wearing red. What colour are you wearing?

Six-year-old: Blue, I always wear blue.

End

On a long train journey, got a Bob the Builder magazine for our daughter. On the magazine's letters page Bob is saying, 'JOIN MY TEAM!' above photos of young readers. Apparently only boys are in his 'team'.

1st September 2011

Spy Kids film adverts. Just in case you weren't completely aware that she's a girl and he's a boy. Pink/blue spy 'aura'.

3rd September 2011

Nephew (four) is very keen on wearing button-up shirts. When his mum asks why he says, 'Because they're pretty. Boys can't wear dresses, so when I wear my shirt I can look pretty like [my sister] when she wears a dress.' He enjoys going to choose his clothes in the mornings.

Another one of these. My niece was having a 'Pirates and Mermaids' week at pre-school. She was a pirate and a member of staff told her mum when she came to pick her up, 'She's too beautiful to be a pirate, why isn't she a mermaid?' Even at age two, appearance is the message.

We get a lot of @GenderDiary material from the kids' cousins. Oldest nephew (of a set of siblings) is off to school in a few weeks. Will be interesting to see how long his favourite colour remains pink and his favourite dressing up costume remains a fairy.

4th September 2011

That post reminds me we need to share some positive stuff here as well as moaning about the bad stuff. Our discussions about language, not using 'he' as default, and seeking out more gender-balanced books has been good. Also challenging those people who enforce stereotypes on our kids and trying to make them recognise the things they say are what shape our children's identities. The thing I've learned most from this diary is that our own gender prejudices run deep, however aware we think we are.

6th September 2011

A friend tells me her daughter had been playing with two male friends, she overheard one say, 'This is a boys' game so you can't play.' They are aged three. Shows a very firm understanding of the differences between them at age three and understanding that there is gender-appropriate behaviour.

I've been thinking about more ways to be a positive feminist parent. Can people share some suggestions here for pre-school books that include characters that REALLY depart from gender stereotypes, also are there any books with LGBT characters, particularly parents?

MT @BurlyQEinstein: *The Shy Creatures* by David Mack is brilliant.

RT @RosamundUrwin: *The Paperbag Princess*.

RT @RevDebra: Books for small children with LG parents: *Heather has Two Mommies* and *Daddy's Roomate* were favourites of mine when mine were little. Also *My Princess Boy* and *Free to Be… You and Me* is a classic with some great stories.

19th September 2011

The @GenderDiary family are very busy with us both back at work now. At the weekend we were at a third birthday party with a kids' entertainer. Prizes and treats for musical bumps as follows: stickers and balloon dogs for girls, bouncy balls and balloon swords for boys. Our daughter was the only girl to be given a sword. Later I saw another girl had got hold of one and was playing with the boys. I'm not a fan of weapons but boys are clearly expected to be.

27th September 2011

Out with dads last night, two of whom have kids just starting school. One a daughter, one a son. Both are asked how the kids are settling in. No more questions to the dad with a daughter but the one with a son is asked if the boy has a girlfriend yet, does he fancy his teacher, etc. Interesting that even for a four-year-old, school is apparently about sex as much as education. Then we wonder why girls get better results.

29th September 2011

Anyone got thoughts on whether it's right or wrong to point out the gender biases people have in raising their kids? My point of view (influenced by Cordelia Fine) is that small suggestions can alter people's ways of thinking in subtle ways. But done with respect.

RT @leahmouse: In theory yes, but I don't think you'd have many friends left if you did it frequently. Maybe just model the alternative.

RT @Bex6810: No…surely it's their business how to bring up their own children? Why should anyone have the right to judge.

30th September 2011

Overheard at One o'clock Club – A mum: 'Yes, she'll be in dungarees with just a t-shirt or something with a bit of pink. It's OK for girls to wear whatever. But you can't do it with boys. My mum bought him some jeans without realising they were girls' ones with pink stitching, well I just couldn't do that to him.'

5th October 2011

It's Gender Segregated Christmas Catalogue time again.[15] Get a grip retailers.

6th October 2011

From my sister today: using a float on each arm yesterday was called a 'butterfly' in her daughter's all-girl swimming class. Today in her son's all-boy class they are called aeroplanes. Gah!

9th October 2011

Kudos to the Early Learning Centre. In their Christmas catalogue, kids of both genders playing with all toys. Not perfect but better than most. When all kids' toy catalogues have a boy wearing a pink princess dressing up outfit, then we'll be getting somewhere!

24th October 2011

The @GenderDiary family life is so hectic sometimes it's hard to find time to tweet. The baby has had his first birthday now and is walking.

News from my niece's all-girl swimming lessons – the teacher: 'You can play with the balls now. What colour would you like? You don't have to tell me. I already know it's pink.' Gah.

And at lunch yesterday, a friend's daughter says purple is her favourite colour. Her dad says, 'Purple isn't your favourite colour. It's pink of course.' And last week in the library our daughter was colouring with some schoolgirls. The oldest was boasting that she had a picture of a princess and a pink crayon and none of the others did. The reaction from all of them was, 'I'm going to colour mine pink too.' Reinforcement of pink culture happens to girls on a daily basis.

27th October 2011

Today it occurs to me that girls must live with a constant low-level hum of concern about what people think of them in a way that boys don't.

1st November 2011

Just seen a LEGO® advert on Channel 4. It's about fathers and sons building together. I look forward to the one about mothers and daughters building together, because that is a regular occurrence in our house. Don't let me down, LEGO. Remember your advert *What it is is beautiful* from 1981.

4th November 2011

Our daughter's friend came round to play today.

Her: Let's play dressing up.

Him: Are they boys' or girls' dressing up clothes?

Her: Um, girls'?

Me: They're for children. Anyone can wear whatever they want.

She chose to be a bee. He was a skeleton and a dragon.

6th November 2011

We had an @GenderDiary-family moment yesterday that made my blood boil and we were all there to witness it. We were browsing in a toy shop. While there we saw two brothers playing with a dolls house, then later a brother and sister aged about 11 and 9 respectively. Their dad appeared round the corner and loudly asked, 'James are you playing with the DOLL'S HOUSE?! CAUGHT YOU!' Having been shamed in front of us the boy mumbled, 'No I wasn't,' and ran off quickly. The straitjacket of masculine expectation can be very public and very cruel.

8th November 2011

OMFG just seen Littlewoods' Christmas advert. The implication is that only mothers do Christmas shopping? Not in this house!

18th November 2011

I notice more and more how, despite my attempts to treat them the same, I can feel how deeply ingrained my own attitudes are, despite my awareness. I mean in very very subtle ways. If I wasn't so tired I'd try to think of examples.

21st November 2011

Something that is bothering me at the moment is the young age at which children start playing mostly with friends of their own gender. We purposely arrange playdates with our daughter's male peers and they play well, but at nursery I notice the boys' names I used to hear have been replaced by girls' names. By age three they've been socialised differently to the extent that they are very aware of their differences. I noticed the big difference once she started nursery. Until then, she seemed to mix pretty freely. On first day at nursery a carer said, 'Come here and play with the girls,' and referred to the car-table as the 'boys corner'.

One of our followers tweeted us about a charity that takes donations for Christmas presents for needy children and has recommendations for giving girls dolls and boys cars. Well it happens that our daughter's granny was doing this at the weekend and got her to help pack one box for a girl and one for a boy. It was a great thrill when she insisted her granny put one of the two cars from the boy's box into the girl's box, saying it wasn't fair. But of course she didn't insist the boy's box should have hairclips in the same way.

23rd November 2011

A voice message from a relative, 'Really annoyed, [daughter's] pre-school nativity play and all the girls are angels, boys are shepherds.'

3rd December 2011

Justin's House on CBeebies. I like the fact the monster is female. Today her cousin, who likes cuddles, visits. He's pink.

9th December 2011

Watching old films with the three-year-old can be tricky but interesting. *The Rescuers* (1977) sees the lead girl worry she won't be adopted because she thinks she's not pretty enough, as though this is the only reason parents would want a girl. And the mice make a big deal of the fact a female has never been on a mission and it's not really allowed. On the flip side, *Pete's Dragon* (1977) sees the boy sing a song to the dragon called *I Love You Too*. I have my doubts you'd see a song about love sung by a boy in contemporary film.

I tried not to be irritated with a patriarchy-enforcing three-year-old today. Playing dressing up at his house he kept insisting that my three-year-old girl wear a floral orange/pink/purple cloak saying, 'It's pink, it's pink, I'm a pirate, you be a princess.' I said, 'You could wear it?' and he said, 'I don't like pink.' He wanted her to conform to his view of what a girl wears. He kept insisting. Only three years old. Gah.

13th December 2011

Listening to Laura Nelson on BBC Radio 5 Live right now, who successfully campaigned for Hamleys to change their in-store signage from 'Girls' and 'Boys'. Her master stroke was calling Hamleys' parent company in Iceland where they have stronger views on equality. Thank goodness for Cordelia Fine's amazing book *Delusions of Gender* that can dispel neuro-sexist myths about gender brain differences.

18th December 2011

Prepare to be furious, 'Legos for Girls: Lego Friends to be released January 2012' (*Huffington Post*, 16th December 2011). 'If it takes color-coding or ponies and hairdressers to get girls playing with Lego, I'll put up with it.' >> I won't.

20th December 2011

The gender binary toy divide can be ignored for most of the year in this house, but at Christmas it's right up in your face, grrrrr.

25th December 2011

Things at the @GenderDiary family Christmas have been mercifully free of the need to comment here. A very happy day. Hope yours is peaceful.

3rd January 2012

Bus driver to our four-year-old: What did you get for Christmas?

She is too shy to say.

Him: Can't remember? I bet you just ripped open your presents and threw them to one side, just like a girl.

Then: I bet you got a doll and a pushchair?

Me: No, LEGO® and Play-Doh®.

Have been told by three different adults over Christmas that you need to get out the house so 'the boys' can burn up some energy.

Losing the battle against the blanket use of 'he' for everything (especially animals who are not 'obviously' female). We try to use 'they', 'person' and 'child', etc. The four-year-old received a toy kangaroo for Christmas which her grandparents constantly called 'he', even though it came with a book that called her 'she' and had a baby Joey in her pocket. Four-year-old ended up fluctuating between 'he' and 'she' too. Must say though, the book is a classic example of the kangaroo only being female because she is the mother in the story. All other animals male.

9th January 2012

At the park today, on a roundabout with the kids, a boy stops to look at something. His mother to friend, 'He's looking at an ant. He's such a boy.'

I need to make a correction. That kangaroo book did have *other* female characters. Phew glad that's sorted, felt we'd been misleading you ;-)

Just found this rather twee, gender-neutral parable (*The Story of X* by Lois Gould). Odd, but thought provoking in parts. Appeared in *Ms. Magazine* in 1975.

On 10th Jan we've been tweeting for a year. And we're writing a guest piece for The F-Word.

10th January 2012

Going through a year's worth of tweets shows what great stuff people have brought to our attention. Not getting on very fast, though. I'm just being reminded how the Smurf movie caused me to froth at the mouth with rage last year. Seriously, one female character in the 21st century?

When I tweeted about *The Story of X* by Lois Gould yesterday, calling it twee, I hadn't realised it was a children's story. Someone said they had it in a book as a child and loved it. Makes sense. If you're a non-conforming kid it is a lovely thing to read. The story was in this wonderful-looking 1983 book *Stories for Free Children* by Letty Cottin Pogrebin (via @Maureen).

12th January 2012

A text comes in: 'Help! [Son]'s school topic is Knights and Princesses! Are there any "alternative" princess books? Or 'boy' princess ones?' I send links:

My Princess Boy by Cheryl Kilodavis and illustrated by Suzanne DeSimone

'Feminism for early starters: Picture books' by Treasury Islands, 28th February 2011[16]

'Six princess books for parents who really, really hate princess books' by Tom B on Buildingalibrary.com, 11th January 2012

13th January 2012

Interesting chat with our daughter (when she should've been going to sleep!) on marriage. It suggested we're doing something right. A friend at nursery (girl) has told her a girl can't marry a girl but, she says, 'That's not right is it Daddy?' I say she's right a girl can marry a girl, boy marry a boy – remind her of married men we know – or, like Mummy and Daddy, you don't have to get married at all. Says she's going to marry various people at nursery then says, 'It depends who falls in love with you. You can fall in love with a girl or a boy and get married. You and Mummy fell in love and you're not married and that's OK… I'm going to get married, and have a cake.' I say that's fine and I look forward to going to her wedding. NOW GO TO SLEEP. Interesting that she raised it, that she rejected a friend's claim re. same-sex marriage. Possibly influence of *The Family Book* Christmas present too?

15th January 2012

RT @mummumbles: @GenderDiary Is there a list of books anywhere for parents of boys who like ballet and dolls and pink?

Presume you've seen *My Princess Boy*? @mummumbles Will need help from our followers for further ideas…

18th January 2012

Not had any suggestions for books for parents of boys who like ballet and dolls and pink. Anyone?

Yesterday, I set up daughter and friend with a PLAYMOBIL® castle. I passed him a female figure and said she was important in our game when we play. He said, 'Eurghh, I only like knights!' and dropped her. At age three he's learned to dislike any female association in toys. His mother and another were telling me that since being at nursery class at school they've both had invites to play at other children's houses, but both have only had invites from children of the same sex.

22nd January 2012

At a four-year-old's pirate-themed birthday party. Two girls were in shop-bought outfits that for some reason crossed princess and pirate costume. Lots of pink. Entertainer led a game of Captain's Coming (port, starboard, etc.) including the instruction to go 'Ooh la la' when the 'Captain's girlfriend's coming'. Not sure how felt about that. Later our daughter recounted it as saying 'Ooh la la' when the Captain's boyfriend is coming. Not sure what that says but probably a good thing.

23rd January 2012

Jeremy Vine (BBC Radio 2) is discussing the gender-neutral child story from today's *Daily Mail*. Buckle up or, better, just avoid. Here's a piece on the child being raised gender neutral in Cambridgeshire, if you haven't seen it, 'Couple raise child as "gender neutral" to avoid stereotyping'.[17]

28th January 2012

Hi @alexwinterstv we're very keen on you and CBeebies, but could you think about not calling all toys 'Mr (animal)'? There are female animals too!

4th February 2012

Freaks me out when we get followed by stuff like @Choose BabyGender. The fact people want to choose shows the expectations they already have. Finding it hard to fit complicated thoughts about the experiences of our kids into tweets. Got a blog post nearly finished to share soon though.

6th February 2012

I try to keep positive as a parent who wants to see this generation grow up equal, but things like the #UniLad culture make me want to scream!

7th Febuary 2012

I've had enough of reading the Ladybird book *Stories for 4-year-olds* at bedtime. It has 24 pages, three stories. All three stories are about a male animal. The whole book contains ten male characters. The only two female characters are 'the vicar's wife' (she can't be a character on her own, she's just an extension of a man) and the mother of a tortoise, the usual reason a female makes it into a story is because she's the ever-present carer. These aren't stories for my four-year-old girl, Ladybird.

Meanwhile on Facebook a friend has posted a picture of her boy pushing a blue toy pushchair. Comments range from 'It's political correctness gone loop di loop' to someone saying that their son having a pushchair caused 'much debate at Christmas…Grandpa's face was a picture'. The first comment is a joke. However the fact is that boys with 'girls' toys' are still not an everyday sight.

8th February 2012

We've just popped through the 1000 followers mark. Thanks to everyone for following. We really like having this space to discuss this stuff.

11th February 2012

Today, like so many times before, in front of the kids, one of these: 'That's because he's a boy. Boys are always hungry, aren't they?' No.

RT @degrassidigest: @GenderDiary Much like girls, they have this persistent need for food.

14th February 2012

To a half-term activity afternoon run by the council. Excellent event but…first we made paper flowers. Daughter is asked, 'What colour tissue paper do you want?' She says red. Woman says, 'Do you want pink?' Then to pottery. Teacher gets us aprons and says to daughter that she has to wear an apron so she doesn't get her beautiful dress mucky. Yes, because girls should be put off fun stuff like pottery for fear of not looking beautiful. No such comments to boys (including me!). Finally, sewing, where you can make a hairband or a bracelet. Opportunity missed to get boys sewing. (I made a bracelet.)

17th February 2012

If you missed the BBC Radio 4 *Woman's Hour* piece on the lack of female characters on CBeebies then listen again. We'll tweet a few points. Dr Helen Mott (@BristolFawcett) did a content analysis of a day of CBeebies.[18] In 70 per cent of stories, the action was undertaken by male characters. So of 43 stories that day, only 13 saw the action undertaken by females.

CBeebies' channel editor said their research showed slightly more boys than girls watch *Everything's Rosie* and *Fifi and the Flower Tots* (Channel 5). CBeebies' editor said the channel is presented with ideas for programmes about male characters more often than female. Dr Mott said, 'When children are developing their ideas about gender, CBeebies has a big part to play in reflecting back the reality of the world.' Finally, it was interesting to hear the University of Brighton's research on absence of parenting/nurturing fathers in children's picture books.

However I will say the best thing about CBeebies is NO ADVERTS. Adverts perpetuate terrible stereotypes to a much greater extent than most programmes.

So despite being glad CBeebies exists, as there are no adverts, here's some gender gripes. *In the Night Garden* – main characters have a pink/blue binary. Ditto *Waybuloo*. Ditto *Zingzillas*. The time of day we most often watch (7–8am) we see *Postman Pat*, then *Bob the Builder*, then *Timmy Time*. See a pattern? We see three programmes in a row with male leads and that's often all our viewing for a day. Back-to-back male shouldn't be there.

Apologies for very UK-centric CBeebies tweeting tonight. We would be pleased to hear about gender representations on channels in other places.

On the way marketing is training kids to police gender: earlier the four-year-old tells me she's colouring with 'girls' colours' and seems less than convinced (than when she was younger) when I tell her that 'colours are for everyone', as I frequently do. She's mentioned 'boys' colours' and 'girls' colours' a few times recently.

18th February 2012

RT @jakkijax: My four-year-old nephew won't use pink, red or purple in his pictures and looks at me like I'm mad when I say he can.

That's the state of the nation people. It can't be right.

Took the four-year-old to the fantastic Hunterian Museum today to look at a brain in a jar (don't ask). The stairs leading to reception were lined with paintings of former presidents of the Society of Surgeons. Every one a man. This irked me, although I wasn't at all surprised by it. In her play lately she only wants to pretend to be females, sadly. The gender of role models matters.

22nd February 2012

In the supermarket our daughter slips on some spaghetti (call the lawyer!). A friendly passer-by says, 'Where's your mummy?' and is surprised to see Daddy. Because mummies do the shopping or because mummies do the caring for crying children? Or both?

25th February 2012

Sex differences are small compared to the ways we're similar. Obsession with wanting to see us as different makes us so.

29th February 2012

Read a recent interview with Peggy Orenstein which says, 'Girls learn the names of Disney princesses before they learn the alphabet.' On that front I was amazed last week when our four-year-old was given a magic flannel (expands in water, so you don't know what will be on it). It was Disney's Cinderella. She knew straight away that it was Cinderella even though it looks different to the original as I remember it. Extra pink bits and larger eyes. Bah!

1st March 2012

The tweet last night about Cinderella and how she looked in the original animation and how she has been updated has set me thinking about the depiction of the shape of women's bodies. The new Cinderella has those very large eyes, like Bratz dolls, and a smaller waist.

5th March 2012

I'm very interested in the way the four-year-old finds characters in books to choose to 'be'. She'll pick out a person, saying,

'I'll be that one,' and asks me to do the same. She always chooses a figure that looks traditionally female and tries to police the gender of the figure I choose too. I choose figures of the opposite sex to me, or animals, and tell her when you pretend you can be anything you like. She's not convinced. I wonder how far this strong compulsion to only be 'like' the female characters (and therefore what she sees them doing) is influential. Also, if she sees a significantly higher number of male characters, how does this affect the things she thinks about herself?

6th March 2012

RT @catesly: I love how you don't say which of you is tweeting each time too. Adds another dimension re. parents & gender roles.

I like that too. It's exactly that kind of anonymity that our kids don't get in the real world, so it's interesting using it here.

My first visit to a toy shop today. Oof! I wasn't sure if they were selling toys or sexism. Bricks are for boys so even new 'girls' line of LEGO® is in the boys section! Pathetic. But given the dearth of toy shops on the high street it'll be unavoidable.

Thanks for the kind words about our *The F-Word* blog. And as we say, it's been wonderful to be able to discuss it with you all here.

One year of the Gender Diary

For a year now we've been tweeting as @GenderDiary about the ways we've seen people treat our 4-year-old girl and our 15-month-old boy differently. We've learned a lot.

We were inspired to keep the diary by Marianne Grabrucker's book *There's a Good Girl: Gender Stereotyping in the First Three Years – A Diary* (1988). She recorded the experiences in her daughter's life that were shaping her as female. It's a simple but brilliant idea.

When our children were born, people would say, 'Oh you'll see, you treat them just the same, but boys and girls act completely differently, it's in the genes.' It isn't. And Marianne Grabrucker's book was the thing that showed us how tiny little things in everyday life shape our children's understanding of themselves as being 'boy' or 'girl'.

And it *was* from day one. There was no time for either of our children to show us their 'innate' behaviour because they were already being treated differently. Cards, toys and clothes given to them were different, the language people used about them was different, and there's the fact that we could expect adults to handle our children differently and direct them to different toys depending on their gender, although they are unaware they are doing it.[19]

Other people continually reinforce gender stereotypes that are nothing more than glib generalisations, and within earshot of our children.

A defining moment of the year seems to be the effect being a bridesmaid had on our daughter. We tweeted, 'Today we had visitors. Our daughter wanted to wear a bridesmaid's dress she had worn for a friend's wedding. She said she wanted to wear her dress because the visitors "will like me". She was right I suppose. A girl in a frilly dress gets a lot of "Don't you look lovely in your pretty dress!", etc. She obviously associates people appreciating her appearance with being liked' (*14th January 2011*). We don't tweet every time someone comments on our daughter's appearance because we just wouldn't have the time to fit it in.

The fetishisation of all things pink for girls has got to the stage where lazy 'research' and the media tell us that gendered colour preferences have an evolutionary basis, despite them becoming fashionable only 50 years ago.[20]

In contrast we've come to appreciate this year the way boys are quickly socialised into disliking anything that is associated with girls. For example, 'Today we saw the second of two different programmes that had a plot on the embarrassment of a male character because he is wearing pink' (*26th January 2011*).

We've heard many parents bemoan the fact that they've tried not to reinforce gender stereotypes in their kids but still see them develop stereotypical behaviour. They then use this as evidence that gender differences are innate. But gender stereotypes are everywhere and are constantly reinforced. Regardless of our behaviour, our children's experience is made up of so much more than just the words and actions of their parents. They interact with countless adults and children, books, toys, television, images, sights and sounds every day and all these interactions leave their imprint.

The diary has given us a new-found awareness that we want to share with other people. You have a document that brings it all together and shows you the weight of it in children's lives. You can then imagine a child's experience as a sort of wall of sound, where dense and complicated layers are built up on a daily basis to make an intricate identity.

It's hard sometimes not to despair and feel the likelihood of change is insurmountable. One of the lovely things about our Twitter account is that our followers share their own experiences, which we retweet, which creates a forum for those equally frustrated by the way children are stereotyped. Like any sort of group, it feels good to know people share your experiences and are struggling against them too.

So let's look to the future and see what we can do. One of the most inspiring things we've seen is by @bluemilk who has run anti-sexism workshops[21] in her child's school. Likewise a teacher who ran gender-awareness sessions[22] with her class while trying to help a pupil come to terms with gender variance is full of good ideas.

And finally, something that The F-Word readers are probably already doing. Contradicting people and modelling the alternative. Contradict people when they make glib stereotypical statements, offer them alternative views, tell them your experience is different. Small actions matter.

12th March 2012

Was at a kids' interactive exhibition at a gallery on Saturday. They could choose the colour of a slide to put in a projector. A staff member says to a girl, 'I bet you'd like to try the pink one, wouldn't you?' The girl said yes, like kids do, but didn't sound very convinced. Reinforcement Reinforcement Reinforcement.

Smurf advertising = inwardly seething. Smurfs: being female is a character trait, and pulling a sexy pose defines this!

The Geena Davis Institute has done some good research on how the media affects girls. Worth following the #girlssavetheworld hashtag tonight.

13th March 2012

Our 2000th tweet shows even we are not immune. In a toy shop I was distraught as son played with dinosaurs, while daughter looked at play high heels, then remembered that before that he was all over the dolls as she looked at a play volcano thing. #swingsandroundabouts

I don't spend all my time in toy shops. But I'm appalled to find PLAYMOBIL® do those mystery packets in pink for female, blue for male characters.

14th March 2012

BBC Radio 4 Woman's Hour are discussing the power of Twitter to bring feminists together and support each other. That is very much our experience.

Feeling irritated about the lack of female characters in new CBeebies shows considering what the channel editor told BBC Woman's Hour recently. Tree Fu Tom is a new favourite with the four-year-old but I wish the 'gang' wasn't all boys with a token girl.

15th March 2012

Doing this diary has shown me that almost every single thing we do/say/see has an element of gender identity in it.

16th March 2012

I was really surprised to hear this on a nursery rhyme CD earlier: 'Punch and Judy fought for a pie, Punch gave Judy a blow in the eye. Says Punch to Judy, "Will you have more?" Says Judy to Punch, "My eye is too sore."'

21st March 2012

Years ago we heard a comedian do a routine about who decides which animals get assigned to boys and which to girls. It's only since becoming parents that it hits home how crazy this 'animal gender policing' is. I've been noticing it particularly on clothes for boys. Animals on boys' clothes generally look aggressive and have sharp teeth. Sharks, crocodiles, bears, monsters. So you don't see butterflies, cats, ponies, rabbits. They just don't have sharp enough teeth and they're just not AGGRESSIVE enough. It's tedious.

On a related note, the one-year-old was given pyjamas with football-playing monkeys on them before he could walk. Clothes frequently play out assumptions about gender roles.

Toys are the same. So fascinating how it's not the toy but the signifiers on the toy like colour, pattern, texture and teeth (!) that tells the child whether the toy is appropriate for them or not. Free choice? Pah!

29th March 2012

I'm in the middle of making a list of 'feminist' children's books which we'll post here, which may be good for future gifts.

2nd April 2012

Spent an unpleasant few minutes on Clarks Shoes website. It's so heavily divided by gender that you can't search outside boy/girl categories.

@clarksshoes It's a shame that searching for kids' shoes on your website can only be done by gender. Would you consider reviewing this?

3rd April 2012

This great piece on how men and women authors are treated differently, 'On the rules of literary fiction for men and women' (*The New York Times*, 30th March 2012), just reinforces our experience of how boys are socialised from day one to believe the 'female sphere' is not for them, i.e. 'girls' books/toys are 'other' and shameful to read/play with. But as Meg Wolitzer says in the NYT piece, it's the publishers/booksellers who enforce the segregation.

6th April 2012

Discovery of unedited German fairy tales where the brave and clever children are as likely to be girls as boys ('The Anti-Grimm', *The Economist*, 4th April 2012). Ace. Never been a traditional fairy tale fan but looking forward to this: 'The princess slashes her way out of the witch's belly and claims her prince.'

9th April 2012

Freakish coincidence occurred today when @GenderDiary and fellow Tweeter @Keris happened to be in the same castle. Real world/Twitterverse collision.

In that castle, a man at the door told our four-year-old, 'You can dress up as a princess.' I presume he was telling boys they could be knights. Activities for princesses and knights included making a clay tile, and they could choose a cutter for the shape, she was offered a butterfly, heart or star. Lots of others to choose from but those were princess shapes I presume. Next, making a wand and when choosing colours a dad pipes up that he knows his girl will choose pink. Ours heard that and chose something pinkish. All just general reinforcement of roles but today brought home why history is so difficult as a feminist because most images and narratives we've seen/heard today were about men. To be fair to the castle we visited, they had great activities and they weren't divided for boys and girls in any way other than by costume. It was only individual people who chose to direct the children in certain ways. History itself is something they can't change of course, but it would be so nice to see some imagination in the teaching of history in terms of women.

17th April 2012

Going to get this feminist reading list for kids finished this week. All recommendations welcome. Will aim to update it regularly too. And just to say, the list is from pre-school through to teenage, so all suggestions welcome. Older kids especially as that's a bit thin at the moment. We'd be interested to hear whether you edit books while you're reading aloud. I know I do.

An interesting test on school gender policing: a nephew has a school project for which he must dress as an elf or fairy. He has a fairy costume he loves and went in that. This morning his parents reported the teacher said two other boys would be in fairy costumes as well. This evening he says there were no other boys dressed like him and children laughed at him. However they have to wear it again tomorrow and he seems more than happy to do that. I wonder what happened to the expected other two boys. Will request the teacher is asked.

Ah sorry if I gave the impression I'm critical of the school/ teacher, no if anything I'd expect it was the two boys or their parents who changed their minds. But I'm going to get my nephew's parents to ask the teacher if they know why they didn't come as fairies. But I understand the dilemma. Parents want to protect their children from being teased for being different, so encourage conformity. Very interesting though, to imagine the number of boys/girls/parents who are modifying their appearance.

Inside Health on BBC Radio 4 now are going to discuss naming genitals. Will listen with interest. Fandango has fallen out of favour here.

19th April 2012

To the body confidence awards at parliament. I'm the only one with a beard in the room I think. No surprise Caitlin Moran is the first winner. Next award: I'm uneasy about a MAN saying how he hands down confidence to women through his beauty products. Corporate awards are picked up by men. Awkward. Body confidence is important. So is having senior women in business. Gender Diary favourites (and new friends) Pinkstinks win. Dove win the Body Confidence Award for advertising. What do we think of that?

Great to meet Cerrie Burnell of UK Feminista at Body Confidence Awards tonight hosted by ace as always Jo Swinson. Particularly inspired by what Pinkstinks have achieved and looking forward to possible collaboration. Or at least wine in south east London. Forgot to mention Brushed Off. They're very slick and look forward to writing for them.

21st April 2012

This is how it's accepted *and* normal in our culture that boys must be ashamed of owning an object 'meant' for girls, 'London 2012: Cyclist Sir Chris Hoy's first bicycle was a girl's bike'.[23] Socialisation of boys to be ashamed of being connected to anything conventionally assigned to girls can only lead to bad things, right? For everyone. Surely it leads to boys seeing the 'female' domain as inferior and associated with shame. And females to inferior status. I know I'm stating the bleedin' obvious but small things rankle the biggest sometimes.

22nd April 2012

One of my problems with make-up at age two is that it's a method of getting consumers primed to buy unnecessary shit for life, super young.

26th April 2012

In a blog on how the world denies our daughters @lulasticblog asks whether to 'reject all pink, princesses and beauty?' What do you think? It's a good question because we're keen not to encourage the socialisation of kids to see 'female' things as inferior, so it's a fine line between keeping pink toys that reinforce gender stereotypes away from your girls and reinforcing the idea that things 'for girls' are lesser.

30th April 2012

So just a quick tweet about films. Broke the rule about having to see a kids' film with a female lead every other time, but jeez the rain. *Happy Feet Two*, what a mess. From the Gender Diary perspective, almost no female characters other than Gloria who gets stuck in a hole so can't participate in any of the action. There is one baby girl penguin who goes to bring help from another colony, but the action doesn't follow her while she does it, so it's just a footnote in the film. I counted ten main male characters and two female. Adult female penguins only featured as love interests (to be sleazed over) or mothers and took no part in the action whatsoever. Hated it. Only upside to *Happy Feet Two* was the fact that it depicts fathers looking after their children. But frankly I'm being kind here. Baby girl penguins gyrating was one of the big low points in a very low-pointy film.

1st May 2012

Here's that reading list for kids we've been promising. Lots of alternative princess books for those who need help in that area. (See Appendix II.)

2nd May 2012

Happy to hear any feedback about the list and any further suggestions.

RT @EssexMums: Gender-reveal cakes? What do you think? (*'celebrations at which friends and family gather around an expectant mother to find out the sex of her child, through the cutting of a cake that contains pink sponge for a girl, and blue for a boy.'*)

Well the upsetting fact about gender-reveal cakes is that parents who consider the sex of their child to be very important will also have preconceived ideas about what a girl or boy should be, which will limit those children.

Would be interested to hear what you think of Sweden's gender-neutral pronoun 'hen'.[24] I think it's a great idea and so was asking to see what opposition people might have to it. At home we talk about people, person, they and children where possible.

3rd May 2012

Yesterday, 18-month-old's child minder: 'He really loves to dance, I've never known a child who likes to dance so much…for a boy.'

9th May 2012

Queen's speech in UK today. The Government announcing plans for shared parental leave. See Rebecca Asher's book *Shattered: Modern Motherhood and the Illusion of Equality*[25] for why this is so important! What the Government's plans are and whether they'll be any good remains to be seen. But any move towards more equal sharing of childcare is a good step.

Happy to have just used our book list to choose a birthday present for nine-year-old nephew!

12th May 2012

Good idea: 'Girlguiding UK say they are…to create a series of "day in the life" videos, featuring successful women in a range of careers.'

15th May 2012

Another distracting headline for a piece that has some useful stats ('Are dads the new moms?').[26] 'Phasing out…gendered roles of "husband and wife" and "father and mother" and replacing them with the…roles of "spouse and parent".'

Something we've obviously mentioned before is the constant naming of animals as 'he' in kids' books. Am now equally irritated by noticing animals are only female when there are baby animals around. There are not many examples to the contrary. The reinforcement of females only as carers of children and then males being absent is standard. As much as I love Bookstart, our kid was given *No! Says Olly Bear.* It's awful. A father bear is present but the book screams: LOOKING AFTER CHILDREN IS A WOMAN'S JOB! It opens with Mum giving kids breakfast and encouraging them to play nicely. On page five Dad appears to ask who's coming to the shops. Olly is. 'I'll come too, with the baby,' says Mum. She's always seen pushing a buggy, providing food, caring. When they get home Olly 'wouldn't help Mum unpack the shopping'. Her job obviously. She appears on 11 pages of the book, the dad on 6. It's copyright 2003 FFS.

19th May 2012

RT @Keris: @GenderDiary Sorry it's so dark, but… [Keris tweets a photo of a 'cookbook for boys' which has meat on the cover and a 'cookbook for girls' which has cakes and biscuits on the cover].

Gonna say something profound here. See that cooking books for boys/girls photo, I just want a world that has 'stuff for people'. Am I wrong? I just want my kids to be able to *choose* if that f'ing cooking book with cupcakes is the one they want, not be told their sex means it *is*. It's silly to be raging here about f'ing cupcakes when some live with gendercide, but the tiniest things are the building bricks of misogyny. It just means you have to (if you have children of different sexes) buy two. That's all it's about. Making more money. Milking our kids.

20th May 2012

Our four-year-old just watched *Barney's Barrier Reef* on BBC2. Every single one of about 15 animals was referred to as 'he'. It's also presented by a man and a woman, but only he gets his name in the title. I say to the four-year-old, 'I can't believe this programme. Not all animals are he.' She says there is one kind of animal that is always a he, 'Dinosaurs'.

26th May 2012

Just looking at activities to book for our upcoming week at Center Parcs. Fairy and Wizard Academy. Not separate sessions, kids must be either/or.

A book read to our 18-month-old at bedtime is all about animals (*Say Goodnight to the Sleepy Animals*, by Ian Whybrow). There is only one female – a cat with kittens! Of course the animals weren't male when *I* read it. When the four-year-old can read it'll be hard!

Kids' books and gender representation is something we come back to frequently here. Being aware is half the battle. I often look at books and can see it's not something that has crossed the author or publisher's mind. Children are learning through books/TV/films where females are never seen at the 50 per cent they represent. It sends them a message.

On another note, there's a very interesting study by (I think) University of Brighton on fathers being absent from picture books.[27]

31st May 2012

Good report on *Channel 4 News* on how Jessica Ennis being called fat is part of girls' reluctance to play sport.

2nd June 2012

What do you think of this toy, Roominate, aimed at girls? Design and build a toy house complete with circuit for electrics. In an ideal world we'd prefer non-gendered marketing, but in the face of the tidal wave of socialisation into gendered play, is this needed? The question I've been asking myself today is whether you have to work with the situation we've got? Very unsure. As @MituK said, 'It only reinforces gender-segregated toys, but then again, it is a pragmatic solution.' Thoughts?

3rd June 2012

The release of Disney's *Brave* will make sticking to our rule (that every other film we take our four-year-old to see must have a female lead) easier. Yay. Hoping *Brave* will live up to expectations. The lead looks kickass. And the four-year-old will love the bow and arrowing (as she calls it).

10th June 2012

The 18-month-old has started to say 'man'. It's no surprise the word comes before 'woman', which is harder to say, and much less used. But he's surrounded by the word man in so many ways. The green man at the traffic lights, so many songs – This Old Man, The Muffin Man, Five Little Men in a Flying Saucer, I Am the Music Man. All these are sung every week at playgroups and on our CDs. Everything is a man. Meanwhile, I noticed earlier all our (small) LEGO® figures are male apart from the single one our four-year-old made up herself in a LEGO store. So we have a ratio of eight male to one female. The DUPLO® we have is much better and came with women in the packs. LEGO for older kids goes off course. And on the LEGO, annoying that the single female figure was bought at our child's instigation and can only be done in the LEGO shop itself.

The kids' grandmother was telling me why it's easier to put our four-year-old in a dress (while she's sitting there), she says, 'Then they're less inclined to play at getting muddy knees.' When I protest that this stops them playing freely, she accepts this is a bit of a shame. But says girls don't keep playing in that mucky way that boys do, as they get older. D'ya think the first thing you said might be part of the reason?! To be clear, I'm not blaming dresses for the fact girls can be less active. It's just one of the factors in how they are treated differently. Adult attitudes to clothes, from keeping clean, to enforcing modesty (if pants visible), to more interest in appearance, could affect play.

16th June 2012

Language. Earlier at the kids' sports group someone asks me how old the 19-month-old is and said he was 'boisterous'. I replied that he was big for his age. The comment was meant very kindly as she was laughing and pointing out how happy he was but for me that word wasn't right. He's confident, especially when he's with his sibling but they're very gentle kids. I put the word down to shorthand for 'a boy having fun'. The language people use about each of them can be very different.

18th June 2012

Earlier a dress for a wedding we're going to arrived in the post. Our four-year-old got very excited when I tried it on and wanted to join in by trying on a dress and shoes. She stood in front of the mirror, and repeated something she's said before, 'People will like me, like this.' I ask her first if she likes it. I say that what she thinks is more important than what other people think. Then I tell her whatever she's wearing she's wonderful. She agrees that I love her whatever. Then says, 'But some *other* people will like me and think I'm pretty like this too.' I understand it feels good when people compliment her on her appearance but it's so often the first thing they say, so as Lisa Bloom says, 'I always bite my tongue when I meet little girls, restraining myself from my first impulse, which is to tell them how darn cute/pretty/beautiful/ well-dressed/well-manicured well-coiffed they are.'[28] I find it difficult that girls are more aware of it than boys because people give them more praise for their appearance. I can't remember who (but someone on Twitter) said every day they intentionally compliment a woman on something other than her appearance. The intention was to make women feel good about themselves for their achievements/intelligence rather than their appearance.

Interesting or just a thing? So our daughter doesn't have an imaginary friend, she has two imaginary dogs: Snuffle and Sniff. Today I learned that Snuffle is male, Sniff female. The story went that Snuffle was lost, had gone back to previous owner, was a naughty dog. Sniff on the other hand has a pretty bow and a necklace. Sadly I think this is reflective of stories she hears – males are active, females are pretty.

19th June 2012

An Ofsted report finds pupils are encouraged to express themselves and to dress as opposite sex without judgement. The shame about that very positive Ofsted report is the way it is being reported. I daren't look at the *Daily Mail* for obvious reasons.

Some thoughts on our own unintentional prejudices. This morning our 19-month-old wanted to put hairclips in his hair. He was wearing them when our four-year-old came in and said, 'Those aren't for him!' I immediately assumed she meant the hairclips, but only asked, 'What?' She had been referring to something he was holding and she never mentioned the clips at all. Clearly they had been prominent in my mind when I looked at him. But they were unremarkable to her. Good. But not so good on my part. One clip fell out at breakfast and I took the other one out without thinking about it before he went to his child minder. A lot of this stuff is wedged in tight to the recesses of the mind.

20th June 2012

Met the ace Dr Laura Nelson (@DrLauraNelson), who is running the Breakthrough Stereotypes project, at a meeting in parliament last night. It was on equality in science and engineering. There was a group of schoolgirls, one of whom said she had told her careers adviser she wanted to be an astronaut, but she understood it wasn't very practical. All the fab women in the room told her she absolutely could do it and gave her tips on approaching NASA. Ace stuff.

21st June 2012

Have you seen this Atlantic article on work/life balance, 'Why women still can't have it all' by Anne-Marie Slaughter?[29]

You read my mind. Men's role is totally what's missing. She fails to consider what legislation could make it possible either. But I think that's a very US way of examining the issue (to look to business to change), whereas my mind goes straight to policy. I think it's helpful though. Much more nuanced than most pieces on the subject. It's a shame how she asks if men are going to be prepared to take the same pauses in their careers. She should be telling them!

23rd June 2012

Interesting that the 19-month-old already sees the difference between the children labelled in a book as 'boy' (short hair, wearing shorts and t-shirt) and 'girl' (long hair, wearing a dress). He says 'man' and 'sister'.

27th June 2012

Dear publishing industry, What's the secret formula for deciding which pieces of classic literature aren't for girls? [Tweeted with a photo of the Waverley Books *Classic Story Collection for Boys*, which includes *Around the World in 80 Days* and *Gulliver's Travels*].

Some news from the kids' aunt about their five-year-old cousin. He wants to get pink Crocs (shoes) for summer but said, 'I know I'd never be able to wear them to school because everyone would laugh at me.' He says he knows he's not meant to like pink but he doesn't care that it's a girl's colour. Ack, where to start unpicking those sad statements? To sum up: one colour represents all girls, and girls are shameful for boys to be similar to. Our culture socialises boys to reject anything associated with girls, yet people wonder why boys won't read books/watch TV and films with a female lead. Ffs. It must be so confusing.

It's just so frustrating that kids are constantly having their choices prescribed for them by gender. We found having kids was a real eye-opener. If you're finding the same, get involved in the conversation.

2nd July 2012

Gender reading gap 'not biological' – girls get more books.[30] I'd expect the result that girls are given more books and encouraged more. Adults lack awareness that they treat girls and boys differently.

'Teachers who pick texts that appeal to girls, a lack of books in the home and an expectation that they should be playing outside are all turning boys off reading, new research suggests.'

The problem with suggesting that teachers pick 'girls' books' is probably thought to be solved by bringing more 'boys' books' into the classroom. When actually the problem is that boys are socialised to reject or feel shame if they like things associated with girls. Now learning is the area for girls to succeed in, boys have got a real problem. So how about society stops shaming our boys? Then they'll read 'books'. It's very hard to be conscious of your own behaviour. Possibly overcompensating is a good thing here.

15th July 2012

Just remembered this from a while back. A relative with a boy aged seven and a girl of five kept commenting on them pairing off with our four-year-old and one-year-old. The implication was that having gender in common was more significant than age in common. So though the boys had six years between them, they would still prefer each other's company to that of the girls. I didn't notice the kids had this preference. Although the adult would use language and divide them by their games, 'Do you girls want to do…?', etc. Adults can presume your interests and who you want to play with.

@brilliantfreak: What's more, the language implies to the children that they should prefer to play together than with the opposite sex.

@GenderDiary: If you could pop that in a memo to the rest of the population too, that'd be great.

21st July 2012

Interesting chat on girls in sport with Tanni Grey-Thompson (@Tanni_GT) on BBC Radio 4 Saturday Live. She says mothers are more likely to take sons to sport than daughters.

A Twitter discussion on this between Tanni Grey Thompson and Carrie Dunn (writer and academic), went as follows:

Carrie: My PhD research covers this a bit. Depends on mother's attitude to sport, order of children and the sport itself as well as the club/venue chosen.

GenderDiary: An expert on tap, brilliant! So tell us, are mothers more likely to take kids to sports classes than fathers?

Tanni: Think dads are more likely to take them.

GenderDiary: If more dads take kids to sport do they take boys and girls equally? Is it just mothers who show bias? I'd be amazed if fathers showed no bias.

Carrie: My work is on attending sport. Done a bit on participation, and depending on sport, yes, mums don't want girls to be 'abnormal' or 'unfeminine' so don't encourage it.

Tanni: It's hard for mums. Girls doing sport are portrayed as not feminine/different.

Carrie: Absolutely. And a lot of factors create that feeling.

Tanni: Not an easy solution either. If it was we would have done it.

Carrie: Not just sport that's the problem!

GenderDiary: Thanks to you both for explaining. Very interesting.

24th July 2012

This just in from the kids' aunt: 'Sitting by pool with two-year-old on my knee looking at *Where's Wally?* book, finding the characters amongst the pyramids. The girl on her mummy's knee next to us was showing interest and her mum told her it was a boys' book! Wtf?! I said I didn't think it was a boys' book, and that my daughter loves it just as much as her brothers.'

Our son was pointing to dirt on his t-shirt today and the child minder told him, 'It's OK, Mummy will wash it.' Er, Dad does the washing in this house!

I was reading something earlier worth sharing: Head of Podiatry Services at an Oxfordshire Community Health NHS Trust, Philip Joyce said, 'High heels have a long history of social status, sexuality and power. It is not really surprising, by the time girls are four years old they know that Disney's high-heeled glass slipper does not fit the ugly women.'[31]

27th July 2012

Oh Germany. At the Olympic opening ceremony they've fitted out their athletes with pink outfits for the women, blue for the men. It's bad enough for kids. Didn't you see those suffragettes earlier? #London2012

2nd August 2012

It's this femininity issue that stops girls doing sport. Olympic weightlifter Zoe Smith's response tells it like it is: 'Olympic weightlifter responds to sexist tweets: "We don't lift weights... for the likes of men like that".'[32] The article says, 'While Smith was preparing to set an Olympic record for Great Britain in the clean-and-jerk event, men (and some women) on Twitter were busy saying she wasn't attractive enough, or that she was manly, or that there was something wrong with her body because she was so muscular.'

Here come the Olympic femininity police – writing in mainstream newspapers, putting young girls off sport. Unbelievable, 'Women's judo: It's disturbing to watch these girls beat each other up'.[33] Also, the BBC3 presenter earlier did his own bit of femininity-policing when he was shocked that Gemma Gibbons hadn't washed her hair today. Seriously though. That *Telegraph* piece is a hackers' joke, yeah? *Telegraph Online* using *Daily Mail* as a template. I know we're just driving traffic their way. Ug. I'm sure not many youngsters are reading the *Telegraph*! But if parents are put off then kids are put off by them.

4th August 2012

Women's football team GB went out last night, sadly. But obviously lots of other great teams still to watch. Taking our four-year-old to Wembley on Monday! Really impressed by the intelligence, confidence and humour of teenage athletes Zoe Smith and Katarina Johnson-Thompson. Ace role models.

A classic. At a children's party entertainers give out stickers at the end – princesses for girls, dinosaurs for boys. Consequently at bedtime our daughter is arranging all her stickers according to what's for girls and what's for boys. Had to have a chat explaining no one can dictate what you can like.

At the same party the entertainers make much humour from how horrible/scary a (fake) worm is. Our daughter used to pick up worms happily, but recently won't. Also interestingly entertainers make a thing of the 'threat' of male half kissing one of the girls because 'girls don't want kisses from boys'. Now, I don't really want either of my children kissing others willy nilly, I want them to exercise discretion. However I also don't want them thinking kissing is weird or undesirable. One of the ways boys and girls are separated from young age.

12th August 2012

Four-year-old earlier, 'Boys look "smart" in clothes and girls look "pretty".' Well, yes, most people do use those words. Hard to argue against.

8th September 2012

An early morning gender-based encounter. Me (Mum) and 22-month-old spend a lovely 20 minutes in an empty sun-dappled playground. Then lots of men with toddlers start arriving. One tells his kid to watch out for 'that little girl' then says, 'Boy. Sorry is he a boy?' I say yes and it doesn't matter. He tells me his daughter is very tough and everyone thinks she's a boy, and they dress her in blue to confuse people. Then he asks why I'm there because Saturday morning is the dad's job. I tell him Dad is at the four-year-old's swimming lesson and this is the easy job compared to doing the hair wash. An interesting melting pot of gender and gender roles in the playground this morning.

10th September 2012

I'm pretty sure starting school is going to be a rich source of material for this diary. Boys who haven't been socialised to dislike pink/'girls' things' before school often seem to change their views once they start.

12th September 2012

I find myself conflicted between promoting strong female role models and not being dismissive of 'girly' things. Complex thing. It can be a tricky path to tread between embracing 'feminine' things and heading down a path of traditional gender roles. It's often hard not to tie yourself up into feminist knots.

MT @hugoschwyzer: Feminist fathers, feminist sons: A conversation with Michael and Zachary Kimmel'.[34]

Nice quote from last RT that sums up our feeling:

> Friends and family, knowing our views and what we do for a living, repeatedly told us both that 'you'll see that biology really is destiny'. Kimmel noted that people tend to presume expertise resting solely on their own experience, issuing sweeping generalisations about gender roles based on a sample size of one or two.

Doing an Usborne 'Sticker dressing Romans' book with the four-year-old yesterday she said, 'Why are there no women's clothes in this book?' Good question.

MT @day_jess: Sent [a letter] to Usborne in June, [saying] my five-year-old has written twice to ask why there are no girls in 'Sticker dressing long ago' Why no reply? 'Do they think there weren't any girls in history?' she asked. Got an email after the tweet. I had to reply to the email and ask them if they could write to my daughter, who had written to them twice in the first place.

GenderDiary: Did their letter to a five-year-old say, 'it's a book for boys and boys don't want to see any girls in their books'?

RT @day_jess: Essentially, yes, hedged about a bit. And they sent her 'Kings and Queens' as that has women in.

It's depressing that our society accepts it's OK that boys don't want/shouldn't like females in their books. Change this people! Don't tell me boys just won't read books with girls in. Our culture shames boys for liking anything 'female'. Perpetuating it doesn't help.

On a positive note, this book she chose at the library today, *Miranda the Castaway* by James Mayhew, is great. About a girl using survival skills on an island. Miranda builds a system that transports water, through pipes, to her tree house. I think adults often fail to recognise that their influence pushes boys away from female characters.

27th September 2012

Still shocked by the Rochdale girl's account of police failing to investigate her abuse on BBC Radio 4 *Today* programme earlier. It's on *Woman's Hour* at greater length now. So appalling. Worst part is that police told her parents it was a 'lifestyle choice' and they wouldn't do anything because she was six months from being 16.[35]

4th October 2012

Ah, school.

Four-year-old: I wish I was still at nursery with [names two boys] so we can play car races.

Me: You can play races with kids at your school.

Four-year-old: Not with girls.

Me: (Long explanation of why all games are for all children)

Four-year-old: I wanted to play with the boys but they said I can't. But that's not fair because the class rules say always let others play your games.

On this subject. I was talking to a friend who was worried her daughter starting school would have trouble fitting in with the other girls. It reminded me that it is totally assumed that children's friends will be from their own gender only. It's just a given.

At the circus. A gran and her granddaughter and grandson on the row in front. Granddaughter is age nineish, and told, 'Pull your skirt down and put your legs together.' I wondered to myself why we insist on dressing girls in clothes that actually just expose parts of their bodies that we insist they be modest about and ashamed of. Crackers isn't it?!

9th October 2012

14-year-old Pakistani activist who championed education for girls has been shot in the head by a Taliban gunman.[36]

I'm at #demoswomen event at Tory Conference. Not really addressing early years element of austerity, etc. that we care about.

Another spot. Standing in a shopping centre with the six-year-old looking at a notice board. Two large adverts, one for a dancing school with a girl in a tutu, one for Socatots with a cartoon boy playing football on it. Gender cues are picked up from as young as 18 months. It doesn't need the word 'boy' or 'girl' on the advert, sadly.

10th October 2012

Survey by Girl Guides reveals that marriage is not the key definition of success. These co-habitors agree.

15th October 2012

Check out the name of these shoes @day_jess spotted: Girls Bootleg Shoes by Clarks called 'No Playing'. Sad.

19th October 2012

This issue of boys being shamed for doing/liking 'girl' things preoccupies me a lot. It lays the foundations of misogyny and homophobia. We need a sort of Pinkstinks for boys. Macho Stinks or something (!). I'm thinking aloud.

At the library earlier. Trying out piles of books always highlights repetitive narratives – mums are ever-present carers and Dads missing. #Yawn

23rd October 2012

Got a call from school today to say our daughter had walked into a tree. Nice work. Told a relative on the phone later, she explained that girls often get cuts and scrapes because they're too busy chatting. Boys of course get injured 'being boys'. She's saying boys injure themselves doing things, same injuries to girls explained as happening to them. Passive.

27th October 2012

Ug. Advert for kids' build it yourself JCB digger, with a deep-voiced man shouting, 'TOUGH TOYS, FOR TOUGH BOYS'. Just like 'men's' adverts.

1st November 2012

Our daughter has an odd way of putting her coat on – upside down then flips it over her head. Her child minder says it's how a boy would put coat on.

5th November 2012

I [GenderDiary Mum] was a tomboy, and was proud of it. But I think I internalised the way boys are taught to look down on girl things.

7th November 2012

Who was it that was furious about the Gruffalo being marketed to boys only in Sainsbury's? John Lewis are too under the sign 'slippers for boys'.

Also in John Lewis – two steps forward one step back: football boots in a rainbow of colours but only in the boys section.

12th November 2012

Interesting thing – we've never been trolled. I often think it's because they don't know which person they're addressing. But anonymity hasn't stopped some people being bullied – and indeed – outed. So it's not necessarily a secure barrier. I think trolling can be very gender based, particularly for anti-feminists. So they may not know your name but they know you're a woman. But with us, they don't. And my guess is that this throws them a curveball.

13th November 2012

Flexible working announcement [from the Government] today. Statement from the Fatherhood Institute on why it won't work, signed by Rebecca Asher and more.

Girlguiding UK latest research:

11 per cent of boys think it can be OK to hit their partner for talking to someone else at a party.

85 per cent of girls think childcare should be shared equally between parents.

68 per cent of girls believe women are judged more on appearance than ability.

12 per cent of boys say it's OK to pressure their partner to have sex, 3 per cent of girls agree.

Check out @NewToFeminism – who founded the #TwitterYouthFeministArmy getting discussions going with younger #feminists – fab!

Hasbro: Star Wars website, looking for Xmas present for daughter. Choose by 'Gender' button is more annoying than usual.

15th November 2012

Goldieblox® (a construction toy for girls) is what I call the appeasement approach. It makes me feel uncomfortable, though I see the need. Summary: it's easy to feel the likelihood of smashing learned gender roles is impossible so this type of appeasement is useful. Discuss.

I find it hard to compromise on my position that I want to treat children as individuals, not manifestations of their gender. But I also understand that some people live in the real world. My grey area is whether the product helps children whose families are not touched by feminism at all? Appeasement is not my position. But I have an understanding of why some people think it's OK.

Hasbro has only five women in Guess Who? but they don't understand why a six-year-old girl objects. Wake up dinosaurs![37]

19th November 2012

A girl's sixth birthday party at the weekend. Twelve girls were invited. That's weird right? When I was that age I had playdates and parties with boys and girls. The thing is, my folks had an unreconstructed 1950s gender outlook, but it was normal to them that I play with both (when young at least). Has something changed? Six seems really young to be segregating from opposite gender.

Which reminds me. I found this nice book in the library about a boy who wants to be an angel in the school Nativity, *Alfie's Angels* by Henriette Barkow.

20th November 2012

I see Hasbro's replied again to @jenoconnell's six-year-old about Guess Who? having only five female characters.[38]

28th November 2012

An excellent diagram for those unsure about what to give a girl or boy this Xmas. Via the Men and Feminism Facebook page.

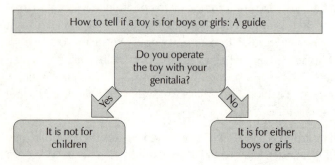

Graphic: Cy Chase and Eva Sawyer

Isn't it the height of beautiful simple point-making?

29th November 2012

RT @MentalHealthCop: I hate the fact we can't buy clothes for our family's girls that don't seem to have pink in.

RT @mokuska: We lost R's hat so Ash chose a replacement, which she loved: blue, with a bear on. 'From the boys' section?'

MT @alexlewispaul: We didn't know before birth, asked mother-in-law to knit with yellow/lilac/etc. Then random people were horrified re days-old boy in [them].

The significance we as a culture attach to colour is amazingly powerful and constraining, eh?

3rd December 2012

Lots of great presents here at towardthestars.com including an 'I can rescue myself' princess t-shirt via @GirlEmpowerment (in US).

5th December 2012

Did anyone notice the most ironic quote in this piece, 'More dads buy the toys, so Barbie, and stores, get makeovers'?[39] 'Barbies are for girls and construction sets are for boys. Or are they?' Consultant on Barbie said adults had been a 'limiting factor' in why girls have not played with those toys as often. *Hollow laugh*

10th December 2012

Ah yes, the Father Christmas boy/girl presents, I forgot this... Our pink-loving five-year-old nephew and his sister were given toys labelled by gender. She was not remotely interested in her pink purse whereas he grabbed it and said, 'Wow let me see.' Their younger brother left the toy car he was given at the next fair they went to. I'm bored of the assumption a child will like a toy you've chosen by gender.

17th December 2012

Hasbro agrees to make a gender-neutral Easy Bake Oven after a 13-year-old wages an online campaign. Sadly, the Easy Bake story reinforces the idea that boys cannot/should not like anything pink/purple. In this case the object is deemed to be OK for boys but the colour of it is not. That's a pretty weird culture we live in, right? And as always the fact a boy 'can't' like/own anything in purple or pink is because of its association with girls. Being like a girl = shame. I don't want to negate the Easy Bake story though because there are good intentions behind it. Gender-neutral toys are needed in our silly culture.

RT @ShelbyKnox: I would say to clarify that [the 13-year-old] was first concerned with having boys on the package and the media made it more about colours.

RT @ShelbyKnox: But you're right – we teach boys that pink = girls, and girls = shameful, everything he should not want to be or be like.

Thanks for that, it's always useful to know the facts, and I think her aim and what she achieved is brilliant regardless.

18th December 2012

Do you prefer a boy or a girl? Yikes to this 'family balancing' in the news. It's tragic. The problem is that people have an assumption about what a child will be like based on their gender. That's so restrictive.

30th December 2012

Meant to say, this is ripe for satirical reviews like the Bic pens thing:

MT @jrwagz: What? Cutlery for boys? (Villeroy & Boch Play! for Boys Children Cutlery Set 4pcs)[40]

5th January 2013

In Boots yesterday. Two shelves. 'Boys' toys' and 'girls' toys'. On the boys' side, science kits. On the girls' side, Disney princesses.

12th January 2013

To the cinema this morning for the latest Tinkerbell movie. Dreadful film (obv), but refreshing to see so many female characters and decent ones too. We went to see the first one due to our rule that every second film our daughter sees should have a female lead. It's a tough rule to enforce, but Tinkerbell films are a pleasant surprise. Like the fact she's a tinker, which basically means an engineer. In fairy language.

14th January 2013

Thanks to everyone for lovely comments. We've tweeted as @GenderDiary for two years and the diary side of the account has dwindled recently and it feels like a good time for a little rest. But we'll still tweet and retweet when the mood takes. Or even be back with a vengeance if the fire is back in the belly.

So finally here are some of the things we've learned from tweeting, blogging and being parents.

The most important one we've learned is to go easy on ourselves. The pressures of pink princess culture for girls and the rejection of anything 'girly' for boys is difficult for children to resist. We do what we can to fight against it, but we try never to blame ourselves or feel guilty about the fact that our kids buy into it. We'd drive ourselves to distraction otherwise.

We try never to force our opinions on our kids but we also don't feel guilty for wanting them to become feminists. Likewise, we don't feel guilty for wanting our children to share our views on equality when toy companies are pushing gender stereotypes and have multimillion-pound budgets that are intended to influence kids way more than parents do.

And remember you're not alone. For all its faults Twitter has been an invaluable source of support, encouragement and sisterhood/brotherhood. We didn't start tweeting with an end in mind but it's been delightful and empowering to learn there are so many like-minded folk out there not just talking the talk but walking the walk and standing up, speaking out and taking inspiring actions to make things better for our daughters and sons.

It's been a privilege to be a part of it.

THE
BLOGS

In the summer of 2012 we were asked to contribute a series of blogs to the online magazine *Bea*. We took the opportunity to go over some of the areas where gender stereotyping was particularly stark in children's lives. But our blogs were conceived with one aim in particular in mind – to be positive. Where many articles and blogs on the subject were big on moaning and short on solutions we resolved to offer a more even split, setting out the problems and the examples we'd found before using that experience to suggest solutions.

BOOKS: THE PRINCESS AND TAKING THE PEE
July 2012

We're aiming to make this column as much about solutions as problems. We love a good moan as much as the next parent (we're so tired), but sometimes that can leave us feeling hopeless. So we're going to try to address some of the things that are making us furious. We're not talking about big changes, simply sharing the ways that we try to bring equality into our parenting. Also this is not a one-way street, we want to hear your ideas too, because, as we've discovered on Twitter, together we're more powerful.

What we'd like to do with each blog is to look at things like media, language, toys, films, sport and relationships, and deconstruct the problems and suggest alternatives.

We're going to start with books. Here are the problems (and we're mostly talking about pre-school/primary books of the kind our kids have seen, but a lot of the problems are universal):

Male characters outweigh female characters significantly

Here's a study from the US on the skewed ratios of male to female characters in picture books,[41] which we can speculate gives children a view of the world that expects females to be less prominent, but not just that, they also see...

Male characters partake in 'action', while female characters often do not

The study above updated the work of Hamilton et al. (2006) which noted, 'Modern children's picture books continue to provide nightly reinforcement of the idea that boys and men are more interesting and important than are girls and women.'[42]

This is a bad situation for the psychology of girls AND for the attitude boys will have towards girls and themselves.

Animals are most often referred to as 'he'

Seriously people, cows with udders are not male. It's one that most of us find very hard not to do. Most people will be brought up to automatically call an animal 'he'. Authors of kids' picture books are no exception. This compounds the problem of males being more important and females less visible.

The historical position of women is presented uncritically in fairy tales

Yeah, we're mostly talking princesses here. If you've never read Jeff Brunner's deconstruction of Disney's upsettingly successful Princess brand, then read it, weep, and consider what message it's sending kids.[43]

No doubt you'll have some of your own favourites, but that'll do for now. So we'll suggest some books here that you can buy/take out the library which contradict the problems above.

You want action? Ladybird do a simple line of superhero phonics readers with titles including *Jumping Jade* and *Invisible Liz* by Mandy Ross.

Spot It! by Delphine Chedru is a simple but beautiful book where the reader has to find hidden animals – and some of them are female. Radical! If your kids love it, like ours do, you can get the sequel, *Spot It Again!*

In *The Paper Bag Princess* by Robert Munsch, a princess uses her wit to outsmart a dragon in order to rescue the prince. The prince, however, isn't grateful enough to run off into the sunset with someone wearing a paper bag. She tells him, 'You are a bum,' and they don't get married. The classic anti-princess book, but not strictly a traditional fairy tale, so how about *Kate and the Beanstalk* by Mary Pope Osborne? Kate climbs the beanstalk, outwits the giant and brings home riches to her mother. Woot.

Finally, a book you can use to discuss the way the world divides us by our gender with your kids. *Horace and Morris But Mostly Dolores* by James Howe. The three characters are great friends until Horace and Morris become part of an exclusive boys' club and Dolores finds herself left out. Soon, she, too, finds her own club, where no boys are allowed and girls are supposed to have fun doing girl stuff. But after a while, Horace and Morris and Dolores realise they aren't happy at all doing what everyone in their clubs seem to enjoy. They miss each other. Is it too late to be friends again? Nah!

That's just a few ideas, but we've made a reading list which has loads more suggestions for the kind of books that show kids there's more than one way to live life and includes books up to age 14 (see Appendix II). Feel free to suggest more books for the list.

And if you like these books but they're not in your library suggest them to your librarian. This can really work, our council has an online form for making book suggestions.

You can also buy more books like this from Letterbox Library, a children's booksellers celebrating equality and diversity. Even better, suggest to a school that they should use Letterbox as a supplier.

Fill your house with the books you want your children to read and give them as presents to others. And for the books that your children choose without your input, edit books as you read aloud – say 'she' for every other animal. While they can't read, this is a temporary solution. When they are older discuss the problems you see with gender in books and encourage them to be critical of it.

Was that 50/50 moan and solution? There's nothing world-changing here, but these are small ways you can show kids the kind of world you want to see.

FILMS: A LEAGUE OF THEIR OWN

August 2012

We love films. Before we had kids we used to have a weekly cinema club, a bit like a book club. We'd go with the same group of friends every Monday night and then discuss the film afterwards over a cheap dinner. Back then though, I don't think we were aware of the Bechdel test. If you've been living under a rock you won't know that it's a depressingly spare way of fathoming whether a film has a female presence in it with these three checks:

1. It includes at least two women,

2. who have at least one conversation,

3. about something other than a man or men.

Alison Bechdel brought the idea to the world with an awesome comic strip explanation of how it works. I'm pretty certain that our weekly club would have been monthly at best if the films always had to pass Bechdel.

Those who haven't heard of the Bechdel test may well want to plead that it's ridiculous and that most films have women in them. We're so used to the reality of the media that we've been brought up with that sometimes it's hard to see what's going on in front of our noses. Bechdeltest.com lists films by whether they pass the test. Here's the bad news. You think of most major children's films in recent years and they'll usually struggle to pass the test – *Shrek*, *Toy Story* and *Ice Age* and all their sequels, for example, don't pass. Seriously, this is not on.

The Geena Davis Institute on Gender in the Media (yes *that* Geena Davis), are conducting research and consciousness raising on the issue:

> They've produced a slew of damning statistics among which the standout one is that men outnumber women three to one in family films and that ratio hasn't changed since 1946. (In real life more than 50% of the population of the United States is female.) On-screen females are almost four times as likely as males to be shown in sexy attire, nearly twice as likely as males to be shown with a diminutive waistline and generally unrealistic figures are more likely to be seen on females than males. Using 2006–2009 as sample years, the researchers couldn't find a female character in a family film that was a doctor, business leader, lawyer or politician and in the films they looked at, four out of five working characters were male, again compared to a 50/50 split between the genders in the real world.
>
> It's no better behind the camera. Across 1,565 content creators, only 7% of directors, 13% of writers and 20% of producers are female. This translates to 4.8 males working behind-the-scenes to every one female.[44]

We're in the UK, and obviously these stats are for the US, but realistically the majority of big-screen films our kids see at the cinema come from the US. Unlike our previous blog about books and the conservative nature of the publishing industry, the stakes are so much higher in film because of the cost of production. Not that that's any excuse!

So here we go, that was the moaning section, now here's some alternatives to the non-representative dross. Here's some great kids' films that have females in abundance and also pass Bechdel.

My Neighbour Totoro (1988): where would 21st-century children be without Studio Ghibli? When two sisters move to the country to be near their ailing mother, they have adventures with the wonderous forest spirits who live nearby. Ghibli has managed to produce films that have complex and interesting characters of both genders for years now. Look over there Hollywood, it ain't *that* hard!

Labyrinth (1986) was an important film for many of us growing up. It's only now looking back that you might realise the feminist message. Remember that important line that releases Sarah from the grip of Jareth, 'You have no power over me.' That's an important message for a teenage girl. Still relevant.

Spirited Away (2001) is an Alice in Wonderland-style tale which sees Chihiro and her family wander into a world ruled by gods, witches and monsters. Complex, layered and imaginative – not things often said about kids' films.

Whale Rider (2002) deals with the pain and rejection that a traditional patriarchal culture can bring. A young Maori girl fights to fulfill a destiny her grandfather refuses to recognise. Powerful and beautiful.

Finally, want to reinforce a bit of that Olympics feel-good factor that has hopefully inspired girls to get out there and try sports? Well, *Fast Girls* (2012) focuses on training hard to achieve a goal, while also being touching and funny.

The actresses trained alongside Team GB athletes to prepare for the roles, which makes it even more ace.

So we never put Bechdel into practice in our cinema-going days, but frankly it's not exactly possible to do the test before you've seen the film. We've actually invented our own kids' version of Bechdel. It's also incredibly simple: every other film we go to see has to have a female lead. (There's a big prize for someone who comes up with a catchy name for our test, I can't think of one.) No doubt you can guess that this is also going to keep you out of the cinema. It's do-able with young kids like ours but is unlikely to be possible when they're older. But so far we've only broken our rule once, and that was because of the relentless rain over the winter (*Happy Feet Two* was very much not worth breaking it for though, let me tell you).

The principle of staying away from the cinema means you're voting with your feet and your wallet. If people go in droves to see new assertive, female-led films like *Brave*, then hopefully we'll send the industry a message.

So there are some thoughts and a few gems of films, but there are many more on our longer film list. I'm sure you can think of some more, so tweet us. Sadly, unlike our book list, films that show an alternative to the male stereotype have not sprung to mind. Please let us know if you think of any, we'd like to add them to the list.

SPORT: I CAN'T TONIGHT, I'M WASHING MY HAIR

September 2012

When we went to an open day at our daughter's new school, the teacher giving us the tour told us what after-school clubs were available. Girls' football was one of them, and obviously we *had* to ask, why isn't it a mixed club? The teacher said it's because the girls feel more confident playing this way. And who can blame them? As Professor Carrie Petcher said to one of us recently (feminist name drop, boom!), 'The boys won't pass to the girls.' I guess it's hard to see yourself as a star striker when half your team are undermining your efforts.

In the warm glow of the Olympic and Paralympic success story, it's easy to imagine that sport is now on the top of every child's hobby list. But there are ongoing sexist issues that explain this:

> Just 12% of 14-year-old girls in the UK are reaching the recommended levels of physical activity – half the number of boys at the same age.[45]

Shocking stuff. The excellent piece of research that brings us this awful statistic uncovered a wealth of interesting information. It found, for example, that boys and girls both agree that there are more opportunities for boys to do sport than girls, and also that girls' experience of sport at school can really put them off it. But here's when it really gets down to the nitty gritty:

> Half of the girls surveyed (48%) say that getting sweaty is 'not feminine'.

> Nearly a third of boys think that girls who are sporty are not very feminine.

Aha! Woop woop, it's the sound of the gender police.

Sport is not feminine, where on earth would anyone get such an idea?? Oh, er, just everywhere. When Gemma Gibbons won Team GB's first judo medal in 12 years, did she get the admiration of every man, woman and child in the country? No, she got a poisonous blog in the *Daily Telegraph* asking if 'women fighting each other violently is a perfectly wholesome spectator sport?'[46] Now the *Telegraph* has clearly set itself on a new economic strategy along the lines of the *Daily Mail*, but the way these papers do that is by writing something that appeals to people's basest prejudices and that they'd like to have confirmed. GIRLS, FIGHTING, TOGETHER?! IT'S THE END OF DAYS! No, thimble-brain, it's sport. Get a grip.

Later, the male presenter on the BBC also policed the femininity of the judo medallist when she revealed she hadn't washed her hair that day. Shocked, he was. Oh piss off, say we. But that's the problem summed up in one small exchange on television. A woman can win an Olympic medal, the pinnacle of her career, and a man can take the time to be appalled that she didn't groom her hair to his expectations. This tells girls that maintaining their appearance trumps the achievements of physical activity. And that's very much what this report found. Being sporty made a boy one of the most popular among his peers. I think you can guess that the same was not true for girls.

Here's another finding:

> Boys were commonly cited by girls of all ages as a reason for why sport and physical activity is not perceived to be fun, particularly in relation to school PE lessons. Boys' negative attitudes about girls' abilities in sport and physical activity were also perceived to be a problem.

The attitudes of the other half of the population are a big factor in why girls shun sport.

So remember our policy, a bit of a moan and then some ideas for solutions. Well this isn't as straightforward as a list of books with girls in. But there really are things you can do.

The Women's Sport and Fitness Foundation, which compiled that research, has been trying to make us all wake up to the growing problem of inactivity in girls. Their #gogirl campaign strap line, 'Our vision is a society which encourages, enables and celebrates active women and girls.' Well yes, that's nice, how do we do that? Well guess what, parents? To add to the multitude of responsibilities that are on your shoulders, you are a big influence here. Taking children to watch or participate in sport is vital. Not just talking about it, going out and doing it. You're also a role model for them in terms of whether you are participating in sport.

The marvellous Carrie Dunn is doing a PhD on this very subject. Her feeling is that access to watching sport needs to be the starting focus. Girls are less likely to be taken to sport than boys. Parents are equally likely to fall into the trap of policing their daughter's femininity by being less encouraging about sport for girls. Carrie's research has found that if girls are encouraged to think that they are allowed to watch whatever sport they want, then they will. Simples, eh? If it's presented to them as a gendered choice, i.e. only for their brothers, then they're likely to see sport as gendered for the rest of their lives.

We've been unbelievably lucky to have the Olympics on our doorstep at a time when our daughter is just old enough to be able to enjoy and understand how exciting sport can be to watch. She saw table tennis, basketball, football, athletics and the modern pentathlon, with disabled and able-bodied athletes competing. We hope it's something that will stay with her for the rest of her life. But will it make her more likely to take part in sport?

Carrie wrote that despite growing up with great role models like Sally Gunnell and Liz McColgan, she still hated sport at school.[47] It's true, sports role models don't necessarily have the effect of changing our physical behaviour. But here's where we hope that their power to influence can work in other ways.

Athletes like Zoe Smith, Nicola Adams, Katarina Johnson-Thompson and Laura Robson are smart, witty, confident and incredibly good at standing up to a world that has ridiculous expectations of them because they are women. Zoe Smith wrote the most fantastic blog post in response to tweets criticising her appearance as 'manly'. She wrote,

> What makes you think we actually give a toss that you, personally, do not find us attractive?... We, as any women with an ounce of self-confidence would, prefer our men to be confident enough in themselves to not feel emasculated by the fact that we aren't weak and feeble.[48]

So though our girls may not look at these young women and be galvanised to become champion pole vaulters, what I hope they will take on board is seeing high-profile women who are refusing to suffer under the pressure of our appearance-driven culture, because that's a big part of what is holding girls back. Young role models like these have been pretty lacking. As adults, we find them incredibly inspiring.

Raising the profile of women's sport can only help to dispel prejudices about ability and importance. So get signing the current petition asking the Government to discuss the state of women's sport in the House of Commons and to consider making broadcasters obligated to show women's sport. The petition was delivered to the Department for Culture, Media & Sport.[49]

But the most important point in the area of raising the profile, audiences and television coverage of women's sport? Take your sons to watch it, because it's their attitudes that are part of this problem.

SCHOOL: NEVER TOO YOUNG TO LEARN

October 2012

Ah school, the best days of your life. Our four-year-old has just started school. Here's a typical conversation when she gets picked up at the end of the day:

Parent: What did you learn today at school, darling?

Four-year-old: Oh you know, just the usual reinforcing of traditional gender roles through a complex combination of adults' different treatment of children depending on their gender, and peers who police my behaviour to make sure I don't break out of stereotypical behaviour, and that. Oh, and we did some clay modelling and I made a snail.

Parent: Great, did you remember to bring your PE kit home?

Yes, for the gender-concerned parent, school is the final frontier in exposing your child to the world as it really is. We've heard many, many times from followers whose kids did not conform or particularly take note of the 'things that are for girls' and the 'things that are for boys' until they went to school. The most typical is the boy who likes pink. Several of our kids' male cousins loved pink until school had the mean-heartedness to wring it out of them. It also tugged on the heart strings the other day when the four-year-old said she wanted to go back to nursery where she could play car races with the boys there, because the boys at school won't let her play their games. (And before you ask, of course she was reminded that girls play cars too.)

There are so many reasons why school can be fuel for the fire of gender divisions. As the four-year-old so cleverly pointed out, research shows that teaching staff do treat boys and girls differently. In a 2006 UK research paper of children aged 7–8 and their teachers, they found, 'Whilst the pupils believed their teachers treated them in a fair and just manner, three-quarters of the teachers interviewed believed they did or should respond differently to pupils according to gender.'[50]

And to those that think it's necessary because girls and boys (yes all of them, because every single girl is the same as every single other girl, yah?) learn in different ways, read the conclusions of that paper.

So what's to do? Well overthrow the patriarchy first and foremost, obv, but if that doesn't come off before half term, here's our suggestions for ways you can get some badly needed lessons about sexism into a school near you.

A blog post by the excellent @bluemilk describes her experience of running an anti-sexism session in her daughter's school class of five- and six-year-olds.[51] She's not a teacher but was asked if she'd be interested in doing it. Our daughter's school has similarly asked parents if they'd like to present anything to classes that they have a particular interest in. If you get the same opportunity in your kids' schools then grab it with both hands. @bluemilk describes a brilliant set of photos and questions she used to challenge the kids' assumptions about gender, for example:

> The kids were really receptive and by the conclusion of the workshop were readily able to spot sexism in toy catalogues presented to them and were happily repeating phrases in their analysis that I'd been using throughout the workshop, like 'colours are for everyone', 'feelings are for everyone' and 'toys are for everyone'.

Do read it and even if you don't do something as big as a workshop, it will give you lots of great ideas for things to say to kids when you want to challenge something they say that is sexist.

Ditto this piece, 'It's Okay to be Neither' by Melissa Bollow Tempel, a teacher who had a kid in her class who presented with gender variance.[52] She similarly worked on sessions that used photos and questions to challenge assumptions and is well worth plundering ideas from.

A more formal way of getting this stuff into your kid's school could be Laura Nelson's Breakthrough Gender Stereotypes Project which has completed an initial trial in a school with nine- and ten-year-olds, holding two weeks of gender stereotypes awareness lessons and includes elements of science, geography, history, politics and sociology. The website says, 'If you work in a school, or indeed if you work with children who you think would benefit from these lessons, we would love to hear from you.'[53]

Finally, the Astell Project is 'a campaign and community of activists and educators which aims to get Women and Gender Studies introduced into schools for 13 to 15-year-old girls and boys'. Which is an ambitious aim in the current education climate. You can help them by signing their petition.[54]

Now in previous blogs we've usually had a resource for you to draw on, and we'd like to have a template for something similar to the parent-led workshops mentioned above, but the dog ate it. Hopefully we'll get that handed in to you in the coming weeks, but in the meantime, as usual, any ideas you can share with us to add to this resource would be gratefully received. Our previous experience of compiling lists and so on is that we're stronger when we put our heads together to use our collective wisdom. Yes, some of you guys clearly picked up a lot in school, but what you managed to shake off was the idea that your gender defined the things you would think. How clever of you! But we all know it's not that easy. So let's try and give our kids the head start that we never had.

LANGUAGE: ARE YOU A PEOPLE PERSON?

November 2012

> For me, words are a form of action, capable of influencing change. Their articulation represents a complete, lived experience. (Ingrid Bengis)[55]

Words. Dontcha just love 'em? But sometimes the 140 characters of Twitter are just too short to record things that happen to our kids because of their gender. Here's a slightly longer story that happened at the weekend that really sums up why we keep a diary about these things.

We were visiting the playground of an aeroplane museum with the children's cousins. Five kids, aged 2–5. Two girls, three boys.

Things that were said by an adult with us:

About a remote-controlled aeroplane, 'Look at the aeroplane doing stunts, he's obviously having a wonderful time. Look at him go. He's really enjoying himself.'

To oldest boy child, by name, specifically, 'Can you see the engines in there, behind the propellers? That's what makes the plane fly. Can you see all the parts inside?'

To everyone, about the volunteers who run the museum, 'Men love this stuff don't they? They have such a good time here.'

Later at home our daughter tells her cousin she wants a remote-control aeroplane for Christmas. He tells her that girls can't have them and only dolls and Barbies are for girls. Also, he tells her, he hates dolls and Barbies.

D'ya see a pattern here at all? Well do ya? How confusing the world must have been for these kids at the end of the day, when their parents tried to explain to them why *all* toys are for *everyone*!

Yes, the language we use shapes the way children understand the world. Language, among other things, tells kids what roles people of their gender will fulfil when they are older. They can try to kick against it, but there's often someone there to tell them they're wrong about wanting to break those boundaries.

Let's look at that first example of language where someone uses 'he' to describe the gender of someone (or something, an aeroplane in this case) even though they don't know the gender of that person/thing. In Brian D. Earp's recent article from the *Journal of Communication and Culture* on so-called he/man generics, he explains why it's damaging:

This has the effect of minimizing women's importance and diverting attention away from their very existence. The result is a sort of invisibility – in the language itself, in the individual's mind's eye, and in the broader social consciousness.[56]

As always @GenderDiary is here to bring you good news. Earp's research shows that use of the masculine generic pronoun in English has fallen dramatically in recent years, while non-sexist alternatives have gradually taken its place.

Earp recorded a marked decline in the use of the term 'mankind', while 'humankind', on the other hand, saw an 1890 per cent increase (from 63 articles in 1970–1971 to 1192 articles in 1999–2000). 'He or she' (rather than just using 'he') for its part, saw a 1194 per cent increase. It's gratifying that this is already happening. But you can help it along too.

You won't be surprised that we'd encourage you to use gender-neutral language with kids when you can. In our house, we are not remotely militant about it, but boy, girl, man, woman, him, her, etc. are less likely to be heard than kids, children, people, person, them and they.

Those who want to accuse us of terrible political correctness are very welcome to do it, but they'll find that they're fighting against a trend in language that is happening anyway. By releasing as many parts of language as possible from the limits of gender, you allow children to choose for themselves whether something is relevant to them. The conversations that we had on that outing sent our children clear messages that gender was relevant to what we were seeing. Boys and men like aeroplanes, is the message they got. The message we got is that by using more neutral language we're helping to keep options open for our kids, and our daughter will be getting a remote-control aeroplane for Christmas.

CHRISTMAS: PRESENTS OF MIND

December 2012

If you're reading our blog, you know as well as us that products that are marketed to kids are frequently trying to put them into pink and blue straitjackets. Lots of you tweet us with awful examples of what is often the same thing packaged differently to reflect some supposed appeal to gender.

How did we get to this point? Indulge yourself with a browse through pictures of the 1976 Argos catalogue.[57] No really. There is almost nothing that is pink, even among the 'girls' toys'. Likewise there are no pages of fierce, dark-coloured aggressive toys like those marketed to boys now. We'd love to write you a thesis on what happened in between now and then, it'd be fascinating. But frankly right now we just know we want this to stop. The message toy marketing is now sending our kids is that your gender defines what you play with. Hands up who wants their kids' play to be defined by their genitals? You neither?

So this month it's simple, a crowd-sourced list of places to buy presents that won't offend your sense of equality. Yes, it may be a bit late for Christmas online ordering, but bookmark this page for future presents. You may be the only person who gives a child a non-gender-conforming present, so your gift can be really important in showing them something different. Thanks to everyone who made a suggestion. They're mostly UK based with a US round-up at the end.

Clothes

Tootsa MacGinty make unisex clothes for children who, in their own words, 'want to step into a rainbow and splosh through the colours'.

Love it, Love it, Love it, One tweeter told us their kit is 'colourful, comfortable and eco-friendly'.

Toys

Myriad Natural Toys & Crafts, Natural play products, toys and art and craft materials.

Orchard Toys, Designer and manufacturer of award-winning children's games and jigsaw puzzles.

IKEA, Not an obvious place to go for toys but one tweeter pointed out that they sell 'Great sturdy toys, not gendered, pics of boys and girls on the (minimal) packaging.'

This is Wiss, Original, stylish and practical.

Science kits

Maplin, electronics kits that, as pointed out by a follower, have boxes depicting girls and boys.

Curious Minds Science Shop, A science, nature and technology shop for toys.

Books

Letterbox Library, One of our favourites. Their blurb says they are 'Celebrating equality and diversity in the very best children's books. We believe that challenging stereotypes and discrimination should play a fundamental part in every child's education.'

And of course use our book list (Appendix II) for great ideas for kids aged 0–14.

Films

Our film list of course (see Appendix III).

USA

Really everyone should look at A Mighty Girl, which claims to be home to 'The world's largest collection of books, toys and movies for smart, confident, and courageous girls.'

MindWare, Brainy toys for kids of all ages.

aMuse Toys, Creative toys that aim to encourage children's development.

If you're feeling fired up about this then we can point you at a group campaigning specifically on this subject. Let Toys Be Toys have been doing a great job of being seen out and about in the media and pointing out that toy marketing has become horribly restrictive.

That's an important campaign and we're right behind it, but something to point out is that it's very easy to get focused on toys and, though it's important, we wouldn't want anyone to assume that toys becoming more gender neutral would solve any of our greater sexist problems, really they're just a symptom of it. The example set by Sweden is that if you have a culture, and indeed a basis in law,[58] that is dedicated to equality for children then the elimination of this kind of harmful stereotyped marketing to kids will happen as a consequence of that, not the other way around. Shall we all move to Sweden? Or shall we change things where we are?

THE DAD DIARIES

In 2014 we finally took up our rightful roles. Let me explain.

When Ros's maternity leave ran out in 2008 following the birth of our first child a discussion was had about how we would divvy up the childcare from then on. Neither of us can remember exactly how it came to be but it was decided that I would compress my hours into four-and-a-half days, Ros would do three-and-a-half days, leaving three days of paid childcare. From this distance lopping half a day off my working week looks pitiful but we were victims of the culture of the time, and that still persists – that women give way if parents don't want their children in full-time childcare.

By 2014 it was clear this arrangement wasn't working, it was literally making Ros ill. I was as keen as I ever had been to spend more time with my kids but two things had changed since my original flexible working request – six years of normalising such practices, and the Gender Diary. Undoubtedly emboldened by all that we had learned from the experience of compiling the diary it was clear we needed to model the alternative. And so Ros returned to the workplace full time, I spent two days doing childcare, three in the office.

It was an eye-opener. Suddenly I saw the sacrifices women were expected to make not just in terms of ambition and finance but status. You weren't fully part of the team if you weren't in the office as much as everyone else. You weren't a proper member of society if you weren't at work and instead you were silently dying inside at a softplay.

I jotted down some thoughts in a blog. The shadow minister for children and families invited me to her office to discuss it. So I did some more blogs and people responded on Twitter and in person to say they liked them. It was never meant to be a long-term project like the Gender Diary but it was a fascinating insight into what happens when traditional gender roles are switched.

Flexible working is even more normalised now but I like to think there's still plenty of wisdom in these blogs from that time.

First class

I went to the local post office yesterday.

This blog can only get more interesting from here huh?

But then it wasn't meant to be an interesting trip, and if I'd been a woman I suspect it would've passed off without note. Instead I'm a man, a father, as of this week spending three days a week at work and two days a week in work looking after my four-year-old.

The chap at the post office counter was very friendly. 'Got a day off?' he asked. 'Taking your boy for a day out?'

Two things:

A trip to the post office does not constitute a 'day out'.

The woman behind me in the queue with her child wasn't asked the same question.

It was a small episode but it was the most obvious manifestation so far of a vague feeling that by going part time I was marking myself out as slightly odd.

Around Parliament where I work there was a feeling that when I told people (but not everyone I hasten to add) I'm going part time that somehow amounted to an admission of lack of ambition, the worst Westminster sin.

Again I suspect a woman would've met a different reaction.

Truth is, going part time does signal a lack of ambition. For a period at least I'm unlikely to move on or move up professionally. That's true of a mum reducing her hours too. But while she is almost expected to take a career hit in a dubious exchange for the joys of childcare a man doing the same is perhaps viewed as either weak or heroically making a sacrifice.

The way to change these subtle behavioural cues is to normalise men going part time to take on childcare just as it's become widely accepted that mothers may seek to alter their terms.

I'm doing my bit.

Man-ifesto

Since my last little blog I've been thinking about two things. Well, actually I've been thinking about lots of things like Christmas shopping and how to make fudge but two pertinent topics.

First, why is no one flirting with me?

A friend told me when her partner takes their child to a cafe yummy mummies flock to him like flies round the proverbial poo. I took my son to Starbucks on Tuesday and we were roundly ignored. We'll try a better class of cafe next week.

Second, how to encourage more men to do and share childcare.

So, with the second and more serious thought in mind a few policy ideas.

Use it or lose it – the evidence from Scandinavia is clear, offer shared parental leave and stereotypes will persist. Make a part of that leave exclusively available to men on the basis that if they don't take it then it's binned and uptake improves.

And the more time men spend with their kids the more confident and comfortable they'll be doing childcare.

Party conference wives – it's the 21st century. Male party leaders parading their partners is just rubbish. Obv.

Children's culture – watch CBeebies for an hour. Flick through a sample of books at the local library. Count how many women appear in caring roles, how many male characters have action roles. No wonder many men don't see childcare as their role, from the very youngest age that's the subtle and often not-so-subtle message sent by the culture they consume.

Sex and relationship education (SRE) – there's a growing hoo ha over this issue and it's a worthwhile debate to have. I won't claim to have thought the overarching issue through thoroughly. However it certainly seems to me there's potential for good SRE to improve things in the sphere occupying me here. Give men and women the skills and confidence to form healthy relationships and from that will flow the ability to negotiate a division of childcare within the partnership that works for all parties – mother, father and child.

Finally, perpetuate the myth among men that taking on more childcare will see women flirt with them – whatever it takes.

What you see is what you get

This week a man asked me if if I was Swedish.

I'd like to think this was because I was doing childcare like Swedish men do. When they aren't abusing the nation's liberal parental leave laws to go shoot moose instead.

In fact I think it was more to do with the little Swedish flag poking out of my plate of meatballs I'd just purchased in IKEA.

I fear this elderly chap endured a confusing day out at the furniture superstore. Given they put a little flag in every plate of meatballs and they sell a lot of meatballs he must have thought there were a lot of Scandinavians in need of a Billy bookcase that day.

And anyway what sort of a world does he inhabit where people declare their nationality by sticking a little flag in their meal when abroad and eating out?

But that was not the point of this blog.

My son and I were on an outing to IKEA (I know, first the post office, then a cafe, now IKEA. I AM THE KING OF ENTERTAINING KIDS) and I didn't notice another man in the shop who also had a child with him.

There was a succession of mums pushing kids round the bit where they make you buy things you don't want (yes, including me – a door mat and a gingerbread house), each and every child creating, wailing or screaming. But the only men were a handful of builders.

Why does this matter? Because even if I model the alternative my son sees far more women doing the primary caring. And what he sees he'll regard as normal. And when it's his turn to make decisions about childcare it will influence his thinking.

The cycle gets perpetuated and everyone loses.

And that is why more men need to do childcare, and government ought to do all it can to make that possible.

Girls allowed

Being a part-time worker and spending more time as the primary childcarer (or dad in normal language) is ruining my self-esteem.

Not because I'm spending less time in paid employment but because six weeks in and despite haunting a variety of softplays, shops and cafes no mum has as much as cast me a second glance, never mind flirt with me as a friend promised they would. (The fact that if one did flirt with me it would terminally fluster me is beside the point.)

But all these trips out have had one thing in common – I'm the only dad there.

On one hand that's good, I'm properly modelling the alternative. On the other hand I'm appalled that the people doing the childcare and those behind the tills, serving the drinks, working in the kitchens – all rightly or wrongly low-paid and low-status jobs – are women.

I can model the alternative till the cows come home but my children are not blind to the rest of the world around them.

Some of these jobs – particularly childcare – need to attract more status and pay. For others it's about offering women a way up and out.

I want to do something about it, I want my son to see a more fairly divided world (if it must be divided).

Suggestions?

Wrong Wright

Up to my wrists in biscuit dough, sporting a pinny and singing along to A-ha playing on Radio 2, I'm reminded of the friend who recently asked how the whole part-time working/childcare thing was going and quickly added, 'It's OK to say you're enjoying it.'

There is something slightly shameful about a man admitting he enjoys domesticity.

Playing out this domestic scene this morning I thought to myself how lucky I am to be baking rather than working. (Though to be clear I also feel lucky to go to a job I love for part of the week too, but that's not what this blog is about.)

What I didn't think this morning was 'Why would anyone rather be at work than doing this?' Because I know someone whose personal hell would be what I was doing (apart from the singing along to A-ha bit) – my partner.

And there's the rub.

The old divisions didn't, and still don't, work for anyone.

It's not just that confining women to the domestic sphere unfairly limits them, the same is true of men confined to the world of work and macho pursuits.

I'm not claiming equivalence, obviously history has denied women far more than men. And society still does – it's maybe not admissible evidence but a particularly inane exchange between Steve Wright and his sidekick on the radio the other afternoon about the different jobs men and women fulfil around Christmas enraged me.

The point is some men prefer thrusting through industry, some don't.

Policy needs to reflect that.

Men need to admit that.

But having said everyone's different…this afternoon my son and I went to the park and I had a shot on the swings. Male, female, young, old, everyone knows there's nothing better than that.

Giving myself the third degree

For some reason when I was a younger man and fan of the 1980s greatest girl group (there wasn't much competition) Bananarama I was convinced the line in their marvellous hit *Love in the Third Degree* was 'Guilty! Guilty as a gonk can be.' For some reason I thought Sarah, Siobhan and Keren were singing about fuzzy fairground consolation prizes rather than themselves. I was wrong.

This week I was wrong again. These are, unfortunately, not the only two occasions on which I've been wrong.

At softplay with my son I spotted the daughter of some family friends and I said to her… 'Is your mum here?'

The horror.

I had assumed it would've been her mum who'd brought her. As it happened that assumption was right. But I was wrong to make it and to voice it. And imagine my glee if, tables turned, someone had said it to one of my kids and I'd have confounded their assumption.

It may show how pervasive the stereotypes are and that I'm as susceptible as anyone else, both of which are self-evidently true, but at the end of the day I was guilty of propagating exactly the culture I'm trying to alter.

Guilty as a gonk.

AFTERWORD

A few years have passed now since we finished writing diary entries on a regular basis.

At the time we ended on a bit of a down note. Having tuned our gender antennae to pick up on the tiniest interference that others might dismiss as background noise we were worn out from cataloguing the daily sounds and our own fury.

If we felt we were closing the book on the Gender Diary in early 2013 then we were wrong.

Since then we've blogged about new experiences and directions, we've podcast and broadcast our thoughts and insights, we've given presentations about our findings at blue chip companies and to audiences at the BBC and Nickelodeon. Best of all we got to meet the woman who started it all, Marianne Grabrucker, who turned out to be as inspiring, incisive and mischievous a heroine as we could hope for.

And there has been much to be pleased about since.

For example, the publisher Usborne confirmed they will no longer publish books 'for boys' or 'for girls'. Boots, Debenhams and Center Parcs stopped using 'boy' and 'girl' on their toy signage. This work was down to one of the excellent new campaigns to emerge in the past few years – Let Toys Be Toys. Other notable activism that has popped up includes work by Girlguiding, Sport England pouring money into the This Girl Can campaign, and the incredible Malala Yousafzai's Malala Fund. We noted the attempted murder of a girl in Pakistan towards the end of the diary, and in the time since, Malala has become a global phenomenon and inspiration to us all.

Meanwhile feminism in popular culture has also changed. There is a lot less shuffling of feet when people describe themselves as one. In 2014 Beyonce broadcast to millions with the word FEMINIST emblazoned in ten-foot-high letters behind her. In 2017 millions marched in defence of women's rights the day after Donald Trump was inaugurated. Not all would identify as feminists, but they certainly looked like feminists on that unprecedented day of action and display of courage, strength and determination.

The flip side to that has been the rise of the 'meninists' – often boors and misogynists looking for respectability under the men's rights banner. Many claim they are looking for the same things we are – a world free of limits and expectations for boys and girls. The main difference is that they seem to see rights and equality as a zero-sum game when they are not. Those among the meninists seeking to push back against feminism's gains must be challenged, those that simply want to see genuine equality that works for all should be encouraged and embraced.

Whether you count this the third, fourth or fifth wave of feminism is immaterial, what matters is that current activism does constitute a wave with all the power and irresistible force that implies. The feminist tide has risen higher since our first child was born. An idea that's seeped everywhere from the glamour of a pop queen's stage set to the mundanity of a family holiday village can justifiably claim to have become part of the mainstream agenda.

The women's march in January 2017 (of which we were a part of course) showed the strength and confidence of modern feminism. Unfortunately the need to hold such a demo illustrates that there is still much to do.

Ros Ball and James Millar, February 2017

APPENDIX I
A PLAYFUL DAY

In the summer of 2016 we were asked to appear on Kate O'Sullivan's 'A Playful Day' podcast. Kate had already recorded a couple of series of interviews on different themes. For her third series she was focusing on 'family' and asked us to come on and talk about the Gender Diary project. A transcript is below, or the audio can be found on Kate's website aplayfulday.com.

Kate: Can you introduce yourselves?

Ros: I'm Ros Ball, I'm a journalist and I work in politics and I'm also a parent and I co-habit with James Millar over here.

James: Hello. That's me. I'm also a journalist and also a parent to the same children. We're based in London. We were early adopters of Twitter and that's why we started the @GenderDiary Twitter handle and various things have flown from there.

Kate: We're going to talk a little bit about the Gender Diary. Let's talk about your own family set-up so people understand where you were coming from with the Gender Diary perhaps. Can you tell us a little bit about how many children you've got, how your day-to-day works as a family?

Ros: So we're a family of four, we've got a daughter who is eight and a son who is five. They're both at school locally where we live in south London. Currently I go to work five days a week, slightly flexibly, and James works freelance and he does a huge amount of the childcare. He picks the kids up every day. That's a change from when the kids were smaller and I was at home part time. We are well modern.

James: I'm one of the few dads at the school gates these days. In 2014 we switched it around and Ros went full time and I went part time and we should have done it sooner. It's clear we should have done that from the off.

Kate: It's working better is it?

James: Before I went freelance I was working for an employer part time and it just worked better because…

Ros: He likes being at home!

James: Yes I like being at home doing the washing and looking after the kids and Ros doesn't.

Ros: Yes. Someone said to you on the school gate today didn't they, something like 'Oh yeah you do the washing now don't you?' and he was like, 'I've always done the washing! What are you talking about?'

James: Yeah it was bizarre, there'd been a heavy shower just at school pick-up time and I met one of the mums. We were just talking about the weather and I said I had to bring the washing in and she said, 'Of course you do the washing now,' and I was like, 'I've always done the washing. Whether I was working full time or part time.'

Kate: It's so interesting. Those assumptions are so often based around gender. It's really interesting because we had another father on the podcast earlier in the season who does the school run and things and we got quite into that discussion about the comments people make at the school gates. It's quite a different set-up for most people, it takes a bit of getting their head round. It's interesting that you're hearing the same conversations.

Ros: That's the way we're set up at the moment, the kids go to school, we both work in politics and talk about politics a lot and try not to bore the kids with it too much.

James: We educate them about it. Children should know about politics. And gender politics, they get a lot of that as well.

Ros: Yes. Not too much.

James: More than most kids it's fair to say!

Ros: Yes, probably. We're living a happy little life here in south London at the moment.

Kate: Do you mind me asking what was the motivation behind the switch? For some people it's purely practical, either their hours or finances, or for my previous guest he came from a single-parent family and it really mattered to him to have that time to invest and nurture with his own kids. It was quite a clear motivation as well as a financial one for him. Do you mind me asking what was the motivation behind the switch because I suspect it's going to link in to our discussion?

Ros: Yeah, although it is a mixture of things. What are you [James] going to say it is, because I'd be interested to hear what you say?

James: The question is not so much what lay behind the switch as what lay behind setting the family up in a traditional way in the first place I would say. When we first had our daughter for a start there wasn't the same parental leave legislation that there is now. It seemed entirely normal for me to be full time and for Ros to reduce her hours. Over time both the legislation moved in the right direction but more than it became clear that, how would you phrase it, not that I'm more suited to childcare…

Ros: I think he is.

James: Not that I'm more suited to childcare, I just prefer it, I'm quite happy to do it whereas you [Ros] don't like the limitations it puts on you. But maybe that's because I'm a man and I'm sort of choosing to accept those limitations whereas with a woman obviously it's far different because they are having those limitations imposed.

Basically I was doing four-and-a-half days and Ros was doing three-and-a-half so the idea was to try and switch it to do four days each and level it up, after all we're all about equality.

Ros: We are so goddam equal in this house!

James: But when I went to my employers to say I'd like to go down to four days there were some issues and some jiggery pokery and I started looking at job share where I would do three days and someone else would do two days and eventually my employers said, 'We're not interested in job share but if you want to do just three days we could do that.' And that then freed up Ros to do five days and it seemed to make a lot of sense and it worked out really well from that point on really.

Ros: Although I should say I work a vaguely flexible week, I work short hours on a Friday. Our employers have been surprisingly good at letting us do this stuff.

Kate: It makes a massive difference.

Ros: It really does. It's kind of not relevant to Gender Diary stuff but I had postnatal depression and I was really quite miserable at home in the early days and that probably feeds into it as well. In general he's happier at home and I'm happier at work to some extent and we've kind of found our balance now. James almost went to a five-day job earlier this year.

James: I did, for a very brief period.

Ros: Yes, he did and found that he really hated it. So it's interesting you know, you find your way.

Kate: I think there's that assumption, it's something I've talked about a lot with my friends, the whole sort of conflict between who does the childcare, how much childcare, how much you see your children, work/life balance, that's come up a lot as you won't be surprised to hear. This assumption that you're going to be really happy at home with the kids or you're going to be really happy as a parent. There's a lot of emphasis on being happy all the time. And in lots of ways it's the most joyful thing you'll do but I know from the experiences of a couple of friends and from personal experiences around postnatal depression that that's a lot of pressure and you don't always feel happy, you don't always feel it's going your way and having the choice to make different choices about how you then set up your family is really crucial in that I think. Something that's really overlooked in making those choices is if I have a better sense of identity and better wellbeing I can be a better parent, it's just not necessarily that I'm there during the regular hours you expect me to be. It's something I'm constantly saying, I've got a couple of friends who are very new parents and I'm always saying to them, 'You're doing just fine, just do it your way because you are the parent and no one else is.'

Ros: Absolutely.

James: Good enough is good enough, is that the saying? The truth about parenting is that it's really boring, it drives you mad. And even though I like doing it, it drives me mad as well some days. I just did the whole summer holidays, the whole six weeks and it was fantastic but that's not to say there's not times when you're banging your head off the wall and saying, 'Go away!'

Kate: There's never an off switch, that's the thing. I remember having this tiny baby and thinking, 'When do you have a day to catch up with yourself?' and the answer is, 'Oh about 21 years from now.'

James: Oh yeah.

Ros: Though I would say the thing we're finding now with our kids now they're that bit older, the youngest is school age, we are finding a lot more space to really enjoy them I would say personally, compared to what I felt when they were younger. It becomes so much easier. That's the thing we're telling our friends now who are just having babies and having really small children – it gets so much easier, you've got so much to look forward to!

James: But people used to tell us that and we didn't believe them!

Ros: Nah, we never believed them.

Kate: For people who haven't discovered the Gender Diary could you introduce it? That's why I've got you on, to talk about that, we'll start off with a basic introduction and then start tucking into it a bit.

Ros: Do you [James] want to say how it happened because it was down to you to start off with?

James: Yes it was, course it was yes. Basically, the genesis of it all is that it's a Twitter feed originally and now we've made a book of the Twitter feed. It's a kind of project at the moment, that might go in various different directions. It started out, I was reading *Living Dolls* by Natasha Walter.

Ros: Which is a book about…

James: Which is a feminist book and it's rubbish really, I wouldn't recommend it at all. But it mentioned a woman called Marianne Grabrucker who wrote a diary in the early 1980s chronicling the ways her daughter was treated differently to the way little boys of the same age were treated. She's a German lawyer. I sought this book out on eBay, this was around the time our son was born in 2010. I gave a copy of the book to Ros for Christmas 2010 and I suppose you [Ros] ought to take up the rest of it from there.

Ros: So I think when I'd had our daughter I'd always been a person who was sort of interested in gender and I noticed when she was born how people treated her and when I had our son I thought, 'OK, this is interesting, people are treating him differently.' James gave me this book for Christmas and what Marianne did – and we've met her and I must say she's quite a fantastic woman, she's a judge in Germany and she's such an interesting person – but what she did back in the 1980s was, she felt something similar and she decided to write it down every day. You know how you might do if you have a work tribunal or something or people say if you keep a record of something you can really see what's been happening, you can see a pattern. I wouldn't want to say evidence but you get a better picture of what's going on and Marianne wrote down every single day things she experienced, that people said about her daughter, the way they treated her. I read her book and I went, 'Oh my god, this is how I feel, I see this, I see the things she's seeing.' I can see my daughter and my son are experiencing different things and they are seeing different things from men and women in the world around them.

It really spoke to me and I thought, 'Oh I'm so frustrated by this, how can I tell people about it?' And of course Twitter was a really easy way of writing down and sharing it immediately – this thing just happened to me, my daughter said this, my son said this and I feel like they are having different experiences – and so we did it for two years, both of us, and it became really interesting. A bit like Marianne, you start thinking there won't be many things and then after a few days you're like, 'Wow there's something all the time.' I'm always writing something down whether it's when I was in the doctor and a guy said to me, 'Oh you've got a boy and girl, that's so great, he can do the DIY and she can do the cooking,' and you're like, 'Seriously?' and then 'Hmmm make a note of that.'

Kate: Live tweeting!

Ros: I don't want to judge people or accuse people or things but it was really interesting to me how the kids were hearing this stuff and what it was doing to them, what they were seeing on TV or what they were seeing on the side of the bus. The more we wrote it down the more we saw it was all around them all the time. It became a little bit of an obsession, we had to stop in the end.

Kate: I can imagine. It would be one of those things the more you see the more you see. I have a very strong gender radar and I get very annoyed by it, but you have to reel it in sometimes. But you know it's OK. Sometimes you have to stop yourself from feeling that anger, it stops being productive. My first question is what was the reaction, what was the reaction to the tweets, did people join in, did people share experiences, were people quite unsettled by what you were doing?

James: Yeah. Basically, people joined in. That's the big difference between us and Marianne, who had to write everything down and turn it into a book and eventually get it published – that we were doing it immediately and very quickly people responded and said we're on board with this, we've noticed this, we've been noticing this for ages, here's our examples. In the early days certainly that was unexpected. We never did it expecting to create a community, I suppose if we'd thought about it we knew it wasn't just happening to us but we never thought it through that far.

Ros: It was an outlet for frustration which other people felt too and it was wonderful in a lot of ways because you had this group of people saying it was their experience too and they would share their experiences.

James: And also in those early days, and to some extent throughout but particularly in those early days, and I may be off beam and I'm going back a few years and Twitter was a different place then perhaps, but the focus then was much more on what can be done, what we can do collaboratively to improve things. It wasn't just whining, it was sharing information in a positive and constructive way.

Ros: There was quite a lot of whining too.

James: Yeah, but it wasn't just whining.

Ros: After a while the whining gets you down so we tried to turn it into something where we tried to think of positive ways to change it.

Kate: Because that was going to be my thing. You've talked about documenting it, very much just leaving it there for people. If you present it so regularly it's going to be quite obvious the story you're telling but people can draw their own conclusions. There's a simple tweet about something that's said to your child but it sounds like it began to become a force to change and an online community grew around it. Is that where it's still headed? Did you want to make change or is it just what you're seeing and you want to tell the world?

Ros: Absolutely we want to make change and what was brilliant and unexpected was the people we met online, some of them we've met in real life, and what we could do for each other. I think of people like Let Toys Be Toys – if people aren't aware of them they're a campaigning group who are campaigning for children to be able to play with what they want rather than a real pink/blue binary giving certain toys to boys and certain toys to girls. They're a really fantastic bunch, they mainly met online themselves and work a lot online but we've come across them, we try to help each other, we cross-promote their ideas and they support us. That sort of thing. We just didn't expect that and it's great. It makes you feel really positive. You can get so down sometimes with the things you see that you don't like but when you find all these other people who share your interest and your passion about it it's great and you feel buoyed up by that and feel like fighting the good fight.

James: Yeah, the only thing I'd question is the idea of a community building up around us. We joined the community in a way. There were already people out there doing their thing and then we were doing something else and we all sort of joined up in a way, not in any formal way. There was Let Toys Be Toys, Pinkstinks were big in those days, we both work in politics so we had access to politicians who were interested in that sort of thing, there was all this sort of stuff going on and connecting up.

Kate: It's amazing how you can make that change. I do some freelance writing and I think it's about a year ago I was almost apoplectic about cycle helmets with exactly the same function and exactly the same design but one was painted pink and one was painted blue. And the descriptions of the two, the one for girls was particularly offensive, focusing on protecting their lovely little heads while they're on their bike and the boys was like 'aerodynamic' and 'you can jump off cliffs'. I was so enraged that I took it to Twitter and Pinkstinks joined in and Vagenda joined in and various communities joined and The Pool picked it up and published a piece and the retailer was pressured to make those changes. To actually action a change, I really felt like the community spoke and said, 'This is not OK, this is not on that you are defining children's actions and the way they are viewed with your products that are the same product and it needs to stop.' As a parent it was a real fistpump moment and it was like, 'Yes I can actually tackle something that really bothers me when I see it because it bothers me for my daughter, it bothers me for our sons, it really bothers me for our children whose gender isn't defined and that it's incredibly harmful.' The number of times I've said gender is not a binary thing and we need to stop this because it's very very damaging, particularly for that young adult period. I did a lot of work in my earlier career on that and I think that alerted me more than my experiences, some of the opportunities that were lost, the way I was spoken to as a female, and once I started to think about, 'OK what if you don't have a tick box?' and so then you look at it as a parent at this pink and blue and you suddenly go, 'Oh this is really quite extreme now, what are we saying?'

Ros: And that is interesting because we're inclined to think that things are getting more progressive but one of the things for example that we looked at was what the Argos catalogue looked like in the 1970s when we were kids and what the Argos catalogue looks like now, and interestingly there's none of that segregation by colour. So there's a page that's got prams and toy washing machines and things like that and they're just kind of standard colours. I expect they thought girls would play with those things anyway but you can't be absolutely sure. Whereas if you look at it now all those things are pink. And the signifier of the colour pink is this is for girls. Oddly that's really regressive. It's happened recently, it's a new thing and it's strange in many ways. There's lots of arguments as to why that is, is it marketing – they get to sell two of everything if they sell it in pink and blue because you won't hand down the colour that's not 'for' them?

James: Capitalism. It always sounds terribly hoity toity but actually when you do start drilling down into it you do go, maybe capitalism is part of the problem.

Kate: It's basic logic, why sell one thing when you can sell two? It's a bit of a no-brainer really isn't it? And I do think, something that really bothers me and I've been guilty of this as well, pink became demonised for me. I went to the end of the earth to get a blue buggy, a little play pram for my daughter. She was not having a pink one. And you know what, despite my best efforts – very gender-neutral clothes, very clear I was fierce about any princess activity going on – she is in full grip of princess mode right now. And I thought, 'You know what, instead of demonising it – I've made it forbidden fruit – I need to stop and I need to just let her express herself and let her make the critical choices.' Yes that might be what's presented around her and yes I can try to be the agent for change, when I wrote that piece and worked online with people, but you know I need to work with her too. She needs to be able to make free choices and sometimes she's going to want to explore some of that heavily gendered stuff and my hope would be that she's going to realise at some point that it is heavily gendered and that there needs to be other ways of doing things for her and for her friends. But I can't do that by demonising pink, that's the biggest lesson I've learned in the last year. It was quite a shock to me what I'd done and it sort of made me think about what I'm actually upset about and let's explore that.

Ros: Yeah, yeah good point. And I think some people don't do that. I was very similar to that. I was really – that really tedious word – tomboyish myself as a child and I wore boys' clothes at some points and I was all Scalextric and not 'girls' toys' and I was determined we were not going to have pink to some extent but I realised we had to readdress that because I realised when we say we hate pink things to some extent it's a kind of misogyny, it's girls' things are inferior, if they are girls' things. I really had to do an about-turn on that stuff because I found that if I say, 'No you can't have that,' what am I saying to her? Am I saying, 'Girls are bad, girls' things are shameful'? So I went through a similar experience myself. I think a lot of people thought we were trying to bring our kids up gender neutral or something, as if that's possible – that's not possible, the world is full of gendered things – but we just had a great big range of anything.

James: We're also too lazy to bring up kids gender neutral. You can try to bring kids up gender neutral but it's just…

Ros: If you don't let them out the house maybe.

James: It involves a huge amount of effort and fair play to people that do but it wasn't for us.

Ros: I think they're very brave.

James: You've got to understand we're not communists here and I don't want to go all communist but at the same time you've got to understand your little girl is going to want princess stuff because you are up against the entire toy industry and a good chunk of society that says this is what you're going to do, and you can't win. But like you say, what you've got to do is educate them, model the alternative and show and give them the tools to apply some critical thought and think, 'Why am I doing this? Are there alternatives? Is it OK if I don't want to do this?' and all that sort of stuff.

Ros: And as James said we model the alternative in this house. You can not give your daughter pink princess dresses to your heart's content but if you're still modelling a 1950s lifestyle in the house what difference does that make?

James: But having said that there are three Barbies still hiding at the back of the cupboard upstairs. Our daughter got given a pack of three Barbies when she was age three and we weren't having that and they got banished to the back of her cupboard.

Ros: She's got some other Barbies now.

James: She does but they are still up there, still banished behind some pillows.

Kate: We have some things that might get kicked under the sofa and forgotten about and then make it into the next charity bag. Part of it is not just the gender thing but I really don't like the unhealthy body stereotypes that are pushed. What I love about my daughter at the moment is that she's a good all-rounder, she loves counting and she loves music and she loves dancing and she loves writing. She doesn't have this sense that nothing is for her. And she delights in being naked, it's the best thing in the world. The number of times I watch her and think, 'How do I keep that? How do I keep that confidence?' The world is full of possibilities for her. I felt like I died a bit inside the first time she said, 'I can't do that, that's for boys,' and I just thought, 'Where did you get that message?' and I just felt really sad.

I had a previous child minder who was very upset about the idea, I made it very clear I didn't like this princess thing, and she used to put her princess dress on her peg because she thought I was depriving my child. She was like, 'She needs to know she's a girl,' and I was like, 'I'm fairly sure she knows she's a girl, I don't think it's about the dress. We may need to talk biology at some point and the difference between gender and biology.' It was one of those moments where I realised I was up against other people's expectations and I realised we have our own hang-ups.

I spent a long time talking to the child minder about it and I realised she had a lot of body issues, she had a lot of issues around her femininity and how she felt about it. We had this huge explosion one day when my daughter came home, she was toilet training and she was wiping herself and she had been taught to call her body parts the flower and I just went, 'I'm sorry?' I didn't really understand why it had happened so when I went in and talked to my child minder she said, 'Well, she can't just say things,' so I said to her, 'I'm going to ask you a question and I'm not being aggressive but can you name your body parts without blushing or feeling embarrassed?' And it was very clear that she couldn't so I was like, 'OK I understand where this is coming from,' and I realised I needed to dial back my feelings because I feel quite strongly about certain things like body parts and she should have a positive body image but actually not everyone is there is what I realised, and not that I'm so ahead of this other person, it's just that we're all in different places and we all have to be able to get by day to day feeling we can look after someone else's child or our own child whoever that is or go about our day-to-day lives without too many hang-ups however we do that. That's the secret isn't it? I need to work out how to plant that into my daughter: just get through the day without hang-ups. I would feel quite happy.

James: That's an interesting point because we've been talking about toys and obviously toys are massive to kids. Let Toys Be Toys are great but you can go down a toy cul-de-sac and think that's purely where kids get their gender ideas from but it's a much wider spectrum and actually the issue of, whatever you call them, private parts?

Kate: Yes, what do you call them on a podcast?

Ros: There's a bit in the book about this.

James: Our daughter was told to refer to her vulva, which has caused a few faces among grandparents and stuff. But with our son we've never gone to the same lengths to get him to refer to his penis. He has a winkie because that's funny basically.

Kate: That's really interesting.

James: That's the thing with all this stuff, you have to realise your own failings.

Ros: Absolutely, one of our learnings from the whole project very much is we're not judging anyone else, in fact we're judging ourselves quite harshly. In fact lots of things we learned were about our own behaviours and the things we do that affect our kids.

Kate: I think it's about being human. I imagine early on it's possible to get quite hung up on these things and see everything through that lens and then actually you start second guessing yourself as a parent. For most people the ability to not second guess themselves is actually so empowering and to be able to just get on and be the parent they can be and be interacting. I remember my friend made a decision I really admire to never compliment a little girl on the way she looks because she remembers as a child feeling her looks were valued far more than anything else. But she loved books so she'll start a conversation by asking what a child is reading at the moment for example, and she's really great at talking to children but I said to her, 'But sometimes it's OK, sometimes I like to hear how I look,' and she said, 'Yes I guess I've gone too far the other way.' It was just really nice that we were chatting about it and we go so far into how we feel about something as adults, and this idea that something used to drive me mad when I was a kid so I'm not going to do that and when you're a parent you catch yourself doing all of those things.

Ros: Absolutely. Again we mustn't be too hard on ourselves but absolutely we found that. It's in the diary quite a few times that when our daughter was around three, in fact it was the day our son was born, she was a bridesmaid. We had him at two or three in the morning...

James: 3.15! I don't suppose you remember the exact time!

Ros: No I don't remember. We were due at a very dear friend's wedding the next day and obviously I didn't go but I told James and our daughter to go because our daughter was a bridesmaid and I desperately wanted to be there but I couldn't be. In fact at three o'clock in the morning I was telling the midwives, 'I'm going to the wedding!' Obviously I changed my mind. So she went to that and this experience of being in this pretty dress I could see it really coloured her thinking because there's a few times in the diary and I've got one entry here, where she said she wanted to put that dress on when we had people coming round our house and I asked why and her language was fairly limited at the time and she said, 'Because the visitors will like me,' and I've written, 'She's right I suppose, a girl in a frilly dress gets lots of "don't you look pretty in your dress" and she obviously associates people appreciating her appearance with being liked. There isn't much discussion from our visitors about what our boy is wearing or how pretty he looks.' It happens so young.

Also there's an article by Lisa Bloom saying exactly this, if you can when you meet a girl, instead of first thing saying, 'Hey I really like what you're wearing,' say, 'Hey, what's your favourite book? Let's talk about that.' It's so typical that people talk about what a girl looks like not what she thinks and it doesn't happen to boys, it's a classic way they're treated differently. When you write it down every day you really see it.

Kate: And it works both ways. I remember a little boy I used to look after, he was always a superhero but when you put him in his regular clothes instead of a superhero costume he didn't get comments about the way he looked and that really bothered him. I remember smiling at the time because this has been an issue for me for a long time working in education and with kids and families and things. I was really fine-tuned to it and the difference it can make in the way children behave, particularly around naughty boys that sort of language and the 'here comes trouble' t-shirts and that kind of assumption that boys like to rough and tumble. But I've worked with some really sweet and gentle little boys and that horrified them. I remember one of them was in a real state and he was going to a holiday camp and he said, 'I don't like football and they're going to make me play football and actually I want to do the other stuff with the girls.' He wanted to do art and he just knew the expectation would be that he should like football and be rough and tumble. The guy who led it was amazing with the kids, he was really physical and a big character so they just went wild with him but this boy found it too much, he was just a really quiet, sensitive little boy and I really felt for him on that side. He wanted that value but that wasn't extended to him.

It was such a shame because he has so much to give but he's been pigeon-holed into what's expected of boys and he doesn't feel he can live up to it, and it was a real confidence issue for him that he felt like he'd failed as a boy and it used to make me so sad. I'd pick him up from camp and ask how it went and his little crestfallen face.

Just give them a chance outside of our expectations and you never know what you're going to get sometimes with kids, that's the joy of them. It's hard to do though, I catch myself doing it, saying, 'That's a really cool t-shirt,' or 'I love that top,' because it's an easy way to connect with kids and often they do love their clothes. If there's a pocket that should be the first question to ask: 'What's in your pocket?' That's usually a good opener because they've usually got a rock or something.

Ros: Interestingly on that subject one of our relatives' kids used to really envy his sister's opportunity to dress up for special occasions and he'd really make a point of asking for a shirt with buttons so he could look pretty like girls get to look pretty. It's restrictive for girls and it's restrictive for boys: gender stereotypes. One of the things that came up while we were keeping the diary was an article in the *Guardian* about people who choose the gender of their baby. It's not legal here but in certain places in America it was and there was this article about people who'd chosen whether to have a boy or a girl for certain reasons and there was a really excellent letter from a professor in the UK the next week that said to choose to have one or the other really limits that child because what you're doing when you say, 'I must have a girl,' or 'I must have a boy,' is an expectation of what they will be like depending on what you think a girl is like or a boy is like. And when you have that expectation of them, what if they're not like that? If you desperately want a girl so you can go shopping with her what if she doesn't like shopping? What if you really want a boy so you can play football with him and he doesn't want to play football? It really limits a child when you say because of them being a boy or a girl they're going to behave in a certain way because they're not necessarily. We want them to be who they want to be.

Kate: Absolutely. I feel very sad about it being such a binary idea. I've had the pleasure of working with several families who've had to help a child choose their gender. It's such an honour to work with these families is how I'd describe it because several have been very supportive of the child dictating what they felt their gender was and I thought it's such a personality-driven thing. There's lots of ideas of gender out there but really when it comes down to it we use the word tomboy but what does that really mean? I was a bit of a tomboy but I flinch at the word because it's saying I was more like a boy in my behaviour. There's a lot of mixed messages out there around gender. I'm aware that for a lot of people listening some people might be very comfortable with the discussion but for some people it might be sparking some really new ideas. Are there some resources for parents or friends of people they might have in mind they can use to explore this a bit further?

Ros: Let Toys Be Toys are great as a campaigning group. They've got some really great articles on their website about how it limits kids to put them into boxes.

James: The resources that we've put together are a book list (see Appendix II) and a film list (see Appendix III) mainly not gender neutral, but they challenge the gender norms. That's a good way to go about it. You can't sit and say to people, 'You're an idiot, you're doing it all wrong.' You know parenting is a very fundamental thing and people don't like to be told they're doing it wrong.

Ros: I know I don't!

James: And most of the time they're not doing it wrong, wrong is not the word. As you say it might trigger some uncomfortable thoughts. The story I tell when we do presentations about this is that I used to play football and after the football game we'd go to the pub and after a while I didn't get invited to the pub quite so much because when one of the dads – another dad who also had a son and a daughter – said, 'I'm getting older, I've started to find I'm throwing like a girl,' and I asked him, 'You do realise what you're doing with that language? If you said that in front of your son and daughter you're suggesting that somehow girls can't throw.' We all know the impact that might have. But when you challenge people...

Ros: They don't like it.

James: Yes. But it's all very well saying, 'They don't like it, bad luck,' but they're not going to listen. A lot of this is about getting a hearing for it. And the thing with the books and the films on the list, especially the books, is they're not obviously different to every other children's book except you'll find that while in a book we had called *Say Goodnight to the Baby Animals* in which all the animals were male – I don't know what all the female animals were doing, they were off having a rave in the field next door maybe –

Kate: They were having a great time!

James: ...the ones on our list are just a bit more balanced.

Ros: So what we did on Twitter after we'd got fed up with moaning was we said let's pool our resources with all the clever, interesting people out there that follow us. We had small kids, we wanted picture books that have female characters because quite a lot of books don't. For example, in children's picture books male characters outweigh female characters really significantly and in studies male characters partake in action more while female characters don't and animals are almost always referred to as he so we got a group of people to say, 'This is a book that I think is great, this is a book that doesn't do that, this is a book that has a female lead.' So we put together a big list of books and it's still available online. And we did the same with films and we talked about toy shops you could go to or online retailers where you could find toys that weren't gendered or science kits that didn't just have boys on the boxes, things like that.

Kate: That would be nice, wouldn't it?

James: Key to this stuff, especially the books, is it's about getting a hearing. It's not about going, 'Look! Here's a feminist book! Read it!' It's just about going, 'Here's a book,' and then you hope the child and the parent will read it, like it and something in their head will go, 'Hang on, there's something different about this book compared to all the other books I've got.'

Ros: And they'll say I've got a daughter, I'd quite like her to have some books with women in them, and likewise that boys can have some books with girls in too.

James: It's just about setting that train of thought running.

Kate: It is hard to source these things. It's something I've been quite careful of, or sometimes I just change how I read it. We've got some books with a lot of 'hes' and now there's a lot of 'shes' instead. And now my daughter is coming up to reading I realise I need to start thinking about this, that was my easy solution at the time. There's quite a nice balance in her screen time especially, that's where I really notice it, the stuff that's marketed to girls rather than boys. But she quite likes strong and brave female characters and I quite often say to her *Charlie and Lola* is quite nice because the little girl is quite brave and she talks about her feelings but actually the brother is quite nurturing and that's the thing I like about it. The brother's quite sweet and he reminds me of the little boy from camp. I have no problem with her really watching tons of that even though it's quite stereotypical in lots of ways but I like the way the roles are just gently tweaked so that I just feel it's a little bit more equal for a girl and a boy watching, it's just leaving the kids to make that decision for themselves.

Ros: Yeah.

Kate: It's been an amazing discussion, thank you so much.

Ros: Hey, no problem, we could go on and on!

READING LIST FOR KIDS AGE 0–14

This list first appeared as a tweet in the diary in May 2012. It's been amended and updated since then and we've received many thanks and feedback for drawing the list together. The most gratifying result, however, has been the thought of numerous kids we'll never meet having their horizons widened and gender perception challenged and increased as a result. New suggestions are always welcome via @GenderDiary.

This is a crowd-sourced list of books, so we haven't read them all, but they've been recommended as suitable to show kids there is more than one way to live life. It's a loosely feminist list with a bit of other gender-related reading thrown in. There are plenty of stories for those who prefer a princess who fights the dragon herself. We hope it's helpful. If you'd like to suggest books to add to the list then tweet us @GenderDiary. We've been given permission to include other small lists compiled by @armyofdave and @treasuryislands so thanks very much to them.

Pre-school age

Fix It! illustrated by Georgie Birkett

A chatty, interactive text and merry illustrations encourage both girls and boys to engage in their first 'real' tasks.

The Shy Creatures by David Mack

The main character is a little girl that wants to be a doctor, but not just any doctor – she wants to care for creatures who may seem intimidating, but are really very shy, just like she is.

The Paper Bag Princess by Robert Munsch, illustrated by Michael Martchenko

A princess uses her wit to outsmart a dragon in order to rescue the prince. The prince, seeing that the princess only has a paper bag for clothes, refuses to leave with her. The princess then tells the prince he 'looks like a real bum' and they do not get married. The classic anti-princess book.

My Princess Boy by Cheryl Kilodavis

Dyson loves the colour pink and his princess tiara, which he wears even when climbing trees. Sometimes he wears dresses and sometimes he wears jeans. Dyson challenges gender stereotypes by being himself.

The Knitting Gorilla by Giles Andreae

It's not subtle, but then it's aimed at kids. When Big Gorilla has a son after six daughters he tells him he'll be big and fierce just like Daddy. But Little Gorilla loves knitting. Can his father get over his own expectations?

Free to Be…You and Me by Marlo Thomas

> The original, innovative book that celebrates diversity, challenges stereotypes and encourages kids to be themselves in a joyful, positive manner, through a collection of songs, poems and stories to be read aloud.

My Name Is Not Isabella by Mike Litwin and Jennifer Fosberry

> *My Name Is Not Isabella* explores some of the amazing women who changed history, including Rosa Parks (it's from the US) and the reader's mum!

The Little Book of Farmyard Tales by Heather Amery

> Mrs Boot is a farmer. She lives on her farm with her two children, Poppy and Sam, and a dog called Rusty. A welcome alternative to the 'farmer's wife' trope. Features a little yellow duck to find on every page.

Where's the Bus? by Eileen Browne

> I'm told this is the first ever animal picture book with all female characters. Can it be true? We're very happy for you to tell us otherwise because we'll add the examples to the list. Young children will love to spot all the buses in the illustrations – which the animals miss because they are too busy doing something else.

Don't You Dare, Dragon! by Annie Kubler

> All Dragon wants to do is cool down and have a little fun, but every time she tries, she ruins it for everyone else! Thankfully, she finds some friends who need exactly what Dragon does best. A book about a female dragon with an integral finger puppet for added fun.

I'm Not Scared! by Jonathan Allen

> Baby Owl is out for a moonlight stroll through the woods but each animal he bumps into tells him not to be scared. Some of those animals are female, which is unusual, and baby owl's carer is his dad, who puts him to bed. You don't often see fathers in picture books.

Big Noisy Machines – Digger by Sue Hendra

> Crucially both men and women operate the machinery in this fun interactive book set on a building site so all children can imagine they are driving a big noisy digger with this fun interactive book that features a sound chip.

Age 4–8 (can be read to younger children)

Handy Girls Can Fix It by Peggy Kahn (Reading Age: 4+)

> A group of girls form a club to fix things. Boys get involved and there's some issues around the roles each gender plays, but this stands out for featuring girls who work with their hands.

Amazing Grace by Mary Hoffman (Reading Age: 4+)

> A book featuring three generations of strong women. Grace is desperate to be cast as Peter Pan in the school play, but her classmates say that she can't because the character is neither female not black like she is. Ma and Nana show her she can be anything she wants if she puts her mind to it.

Princess Grace by Mary Hoffman (Reading Age: 4+)

> This time, Grace has the chance to be a princess in a school parade but princesses don't seem to actually do much. Her teacher teaches her about warrior princesses such as Pin-Yang of China who started a woman's army,

and Amina of Nigeria who led warriors into battle. Grace becomes her own kind of princess.

Mirette on the High Wire by Emily Arnold McCully (Reading Age: 4+)

Best summed up by the first reviewer on Amazon: 'How many children's books do you know where the girl (rather than a boy or an animal) saves the day by doing something heroic? Relatively few come to my mind. I was delighted to find this wonderful tale of 19th-century entertainment fits that bill. Ms. McCully had originally set out to write a biography of the famous tightrope walker Blondin, when she decided to write this book instead. The Mirette character is based on her own recollections of being a brave girl.'

Zog by Julia Donaldson (Reading Age: 4+)

Zog is an accident prone dragon failing in his training but he gets by with help from a mysterious girl. When he has to take on the hardest task at Dragon School – capturing a princess – she's on hand to save the day again.

Kate and the Beanstalk by Mary Pope Osborne (Reading Age: 4+)

Same story as the classic fairy tale except the protagonist is a clever young girl who climbs the beanstalk, outwits the giant and brings home riches to her mother. Basically proving there's no need for all the fairy tale heroes to be men.

Horace and Morris But Mostly Dolores by James Howe (Reading Age: 4+)

Horace, Morris and Dolores do everything together until Horace and Morris join a club that's just for boys. Dolores is forced to join a girls club but they don't have adventures like she used to. So instead she sets up her own gang, open to anyone who's up for adventure regardless of gender.

Girls Are Not Chicks Coloring Book by Julie Novak and Jacinta Bunnell (Reading Age: 4+)

This book helps sets itself the not inconsiderable task of deconstructing the homogeneity of gender expression in children's media. It does so by showing girls are thinkers, creators, fighters, healers and superheroes – not chicks.

Cinder Edna by Ellen Jackson (Reading Age: 4+)

Like her neighbour Cinderella, Cinder Edna lives a life of drudgery at the hands of her wicked stepmother and stepsisters. But instead of relying on the off chance a fairy godmother will turn up, Edna uses her own wits and drive to ensure a happy ending.

Piggybook by Anthony Browne (Reading Age: 4+)

Mr Piggott and his two sons behave like pigs to Mrs Piggott. So she leaves them and they start to change in all sorts of unexpected ways.

Girls Will Be Boys Will Be Girls Will Be… by Jacinta Bunnell and Irit Reinheimer (Reading Age: 4+)

Girls Will Be Boys Will Be Girls pokes fun at the tired constraints of gender normativity and makes it OK to step outside the lines.

Princess Smartypants by Babette Cole (Reading Age: 4+)

Princess Smartypants does not want to get married to any of the princes keen to tie the knot with her. Turns the tropes on their head as she battles to preserve her independence.

Prince Cinders by Babette Cole (Reading Age: 4+)

> Another classic fairy tale with the genders switched. Prince Cinders is bullied by his brothers and things only change when a small, dirty fairy falls down the chimney and starts shooting off spells.

The Tough Princess by Martin Waddell and Patrick Benson (Reading Age: 4+)

> Another princess who would rather be slaying dragons than choosing a suitor. Straightforward but slightly subversive.

Jane and the Dragon by Martin Baynton (Reading Age: 4+)

> No one but the court jester takes Jane seriously when she says she wants to be a knight. When a dragon swoops into the kingdom and steals the prince, they start taking her a whole lot more seriously.

Daddy's Roommate by Michael Willhoite (Reading Age: 4+)

> This story's narrator begins with his parents' divorce and continues with the arrival of 'someone new at Daddy's house'. The new arrival is male. This new concept is explained to the child as 'just one more kind of love'.

Heather Has Two Mommies by Leslea Newman (Reading Age: 4+)

> Heather feels different when she starts school and the other kids ask her about her daddy, because Heather has two mummies. But when the class draw their own families it becomes clear everyone is different.

Clever Polly and the Stupid Wolf by Catherine Storr (Reading Age: 5+)

> A little dated but the set-up of a comedically thick wolf getting outsmarted by a clever little girl is timeless.

The Great Big Book of Families by Mary
Hoffman (Reading Age: 5+)

> A lesson in what families are really like today rather than
> the nuclear family portrayed in so many children's books
> down the years.

10,000 Dresses by Marcus Ewert (Reading Age: 5+)

> Bailey likes dresses. But Bailey is a boy and his parents tell
> him that's not something he should be thinking about at
> all. But an unlikely friendship with an older girl allows him
> to follow his dreams and start making dresses.

The Princess and the Dragon by Audrey
Wood (Reading Age: 5+)

> A princess who behaves like a dragon switches roles
> with a dragon that behaves like a princess and both get
> satisfaction from doing what they want rather than the
> roles society expects of them.

The Big Brother by Stephanie Dagg (Reading Age: 5+)

> Will Dara know what to do when the new baby comes?
> If only he could have a doll to practise. A challenge
> to gendered ideas about children's toys. Funny and
> heartwarming.

Captain Abdul's Pirate School by Colin
McNaughton (Reading Age: 5+)

> This is the story (in diary form) of reluctant pirate pupil,
> Pickles. At Captain Abdul's awful academy, Pickles is
> taught essential pirate topics such as how to make cannon
> balls and the correct way to say, 'Ooh arrgh!' Discovering
> a plot to kidnap the pupils and hold them to ransom,
> Pickles leads a daring mutiny. Pickles is revealed on the
> last page to be a girl called Maisy.

The Princesses Have a Ball by Teresa Bateman (Reading Age: 6+)

> The king is puzzled. Why aren't his 12 daughters dreaming of princes? Subversive (and rhyming) high jinks by sporty princesses with attitude. The ball they have is a baseball.

Rickshaw Girl by Mitali Perkins (Reading Age: 7+)

> Saleem can drive a rickshaw and help earn money for his family. Naima longs to help but is forbidden as a girl. A wonderfully unique story set in rural Bangladesh exploring the challenges change brings.

Matilda by Roald Dahl (Reading Age: 7+)

> At age five Matilda is a genius. But her awful parents don't like her let alone appreciate her. With the help of a kindly teacher Matilda unlocks supernatural powers and uses them to stand up to her parents and the school's monstrous headteacher.

Bill's New Frock by Anne Fine (Reading Age: 7+)

> Bill Simpson wakes up to find he's a girl, and his mother makes him wear a pink dress to school. How on earth is he going to survive a whole day like this? Everything just seems to be different for girls. Popular with schools teaching the concept of gender stereotypes and the limits they impose.

Petronella by Jay Williams (Reading Age: 8+)

> A fantasy book in which it's Princess Petronella leading the action. Wit and surprise along the way as she attempts to rescue a prince.

Girls Think of Everything: Stories of Ingenious Inventions by Women by Catherine Thimmesh (Reading Age: 8+)

> An invaluable counterbalance to the idea that men are responsible for all the major inventions in history. In kitchens, living rooms, labs and garages there's kit that's changed our lives and we've women to thank for it.

The Wrestling Princess and Other Stories by Judy Corbalis and Helen Craig (Reading Age: 8+)

> Six stories, each about a girl who pursues interests such as driving a forklift truck, fighting dragons or piloting a helicopter, as well as a hungry monster, a pink elephant and a magic parrot.

My Naughty Little Sister by Dorothy Edwards (Reading Age: 8+)

> The little sister of the title may seem downright naughty, but not being a good girl is pretty radical in kids' books making her alright really.

Ramona the Pest by Beverly Cleary, illustrated by Tracy Dockray (Reading Age: 8+)

> *Ramona the Pest* shows us a mischievous girl's perspective on the trials and delights of beginning school. In this book Ramona is age five; follow the series right through until the final book, *Ramona's World*, when she turns ten.

The Ordinary Princess by M. M. Kaye (Reading Age: 8+)

> The youngest of seven princesses is given the gift of being ordinary. She leaves the royal palace to live in the forest and gets a job as a kitchen maid. Turns out being ordinary is actually entertaining.

Pippi Longstocking by Astrid Lindgren (Reading Age: 8+)

Children's classic. Pippi lives without grown-ups in Villa Villekulla with a horse, a monkey and a big suitcase full of gold coins. The grown-ups in her village try to make Pippi behave in ways that they think a little girl should but Pippi has other ideas. She would much rather spend her days arranging wild, exciting adventures to enjoy with her neighbours, Tommy and Annika, or entertaining everyone she meets with her outrageous stories.

Age 9–12

Seesaw Girl by Linda Sue Park (Reading Age: 9+)

The setting is 17th-century Korea making this one interesting from the off. Jade is subject to society's rules on behaviour but she wants to break free.

Girls Are Best by Sandi Toksvig (Reading Age: 9+)

Women gladiators, women in the Bayeux Tapestry, women inventors – Sandi Toksvig uncovers them all in an effort to rebalance the balance in history.

His Dark Materials Trilogy: Northern Lights, The Subtle Knife, Amber Spyglass by Philip Pullman (Reading Age: 9+)

Laden with awards and full of ace female characters. This trilogy begins in Oxford before Lyra and her animal daemon Pantalaimon must head to the ice kingdoms of the far north, on a mission to save the world.

The Turbulent Term of Tyke Tiler by
Gene Kemp (Reading Age: 9+)

The book tells the story of its main characters' final term at Cricklepit Combined School. It is principally narrated by 'Tyke' Tiler, a bold and athletic 12-year-old with the reputation of being a troublemaker. Up to the end of the penultimate chapter the narrative is written without revealing the protagonist's gender, and the daring nature of Tyke's exploits often leads readers to assume Tyke is a boy. The story ends with the revelation that Tyke is female and her full name Theodora.

Bridge to Terabithia by Katherine Paterson (Reading Age: 9+)

Even the names are gender neutral in this classic tale of Jess and his new friend Leslie. Leslie changes Jess's view about what a girl can do and be and has a profound impact on his life.

The Tales of Beedle the Bard by
J.K. Rowling (Reading Age: 9+)

This is here as part of the alternative-princess meme. *The Tales of Beedle the Bard* are the fairy tales that witches and wizards read to their kids and which have a role in assisting Harry Potter in his quests against Voldemort. J.K. Rowling doesn't write princesses sitting around waiting to be rescued.

Dealing with Dragons by Patricia C. Wrede
(Reading Age: 10+)

A princess and a dragon lead an extraordinary cast of characters in this first book in the Enchanted Forest Chronicles series.

The Hero and the Crown by
Robin McKinley (Reading Age: 10+)

There is no place in the country of Damar for Aerin, daughter of a witch-woman, who is also the king's daughter, and so she befriends her father's crippled war-horse, Talat, and teases her cousin Tor into teaching her to handle a sword. Aerin rediscovers the old recipe for dragonfire-proof kenet, and when the army is called away to the other side of the country, it is she who, alone but for Talat, rides out to confront Maur, the Black Dragon, the last of the Great Dragons, for centuries thought dead.

A Hat Full of Sky by Terry Pratchett (Reading Age: 12+)

Terry Pratchett's second Tiffany Aching novel. The heroine has saved the world once before, now the 11-year-old armed with her trusty frying pan must go into battle once again.

Parrotfish by Ellen Wittlinger (Reading Age: 12+)

Parrotfish can serve as an introduction to transgender issues for curious readers. Angela changes her name to Grady, and begins to live as a boy, and though his family and friends initially have trouble accepting the change, he does find support from them and one particular teacher.

Dolltopia by Abby Denson (Reading Age: 12+)

A Barbie-like doll suffers a crisis once she realises her fate is to live in a dream house and marry a boring, Ken-like doll. So what does she do? She breaks free, gets a punk haircut and makes her way to Dolltopia, a land full of rebel dolls who refuse to live lives that were planned out for them.

Spindle's End by Robin McKinley (Reading Age: 14+)

For kids that think they are too old for Sleeping Beauty this retelling features a heroine who prefers leather breeches to ball gowns, can communicate with animals and saves herself and her village from the sleeping enchantment.

Shadows on the Moon by Zoe Marriott (Reading Age: 14+)

Sixteen-year-old Suzume is able to recreate herself in any form. But who is she really? A powerful tale of magic, love and revenge with a strong female lead, set in fairy tale Japan.

Zoe Marriot is a follower of @GenderDiary and picked out this one in particular for this list, but take a look at all her books.

Adults' reading

There's a Good Girl: Gender Stereotyping in the First Three Years – A Diary by Marianne Grabrucker

The book that inspired @GenderDiary.

Further resources

A Mighty Girl is the world's largest collection of books and movies for parents, teachers, and others dedicated to raising smart, confident and courageous girls.

www.amightygirl.com/about

Letterbox Library is a children's booksellers celebrating equality and diversity.

www.letterboxlibrary.com

FILM LIST FOR KIDS AGE 0–14

This is a crowd-sourced list of films, so we haven't seen them all, but they've been recommended as having themes that are broadly feminist. It will go without saying that there are never any 'perfect' films, although it's nice to know they should all pass the Bechdel test and then some, and are marked as such. We hope it's helpful.

If you'd like to suggest films to add to the list then tweet us @GenderDiary.

Certificate U (suitable for all)

Lilo & Stitch (2002) Passes Bechdel
Two orphaned sisters in Hawaii are desperate to stay together but they have to prove to the social work department that they are up to it. A task made all the more difficult when a little blue alien called Stitch enters the fray bringing big dose of chaos with him.

My Neighbour Totoro (1988) Not Bechdel listed
Where would 21st-century children be without Studio Ghibli? When two sisters move to the country to be near their ailing mother, they have adventures with the wondrous forest spirits who live nearby. Ghibli magic.

Hoodwinked! (2005) Passes Bechdel
Hoodwinked fuses the classic fairy tale of Little Red Riding Hood with the criss-crossing storylines of film noir – pretty ambitious stuff for a computer-animated cartoon. Well-known fairy tale given a twist.

The Secret Garden (1993) Passes Bechdel
Opening in India in the early 1900s, when Mary is orphaned she is sent to live in Misselthwaite Manor with her melancholy uncle who is often away. Mary explores the estate alone until she finds friends. Together they restore a neglected garden. Mary is ace. And Maggie Smith is in it.

Matilda (1996) Passes Bechdel
Neglected by her stupid, self-interested parents, the remarkably intelligent Matilda develops telekinetic powers. The original book is on our booklist, and though the film is not as good as the book, it's worth a mention because the main character is a strong, confident and brilliant girl.

The Hideaways (1973) Not Bechdel listed
A young brother and sister run away from home and hide out in the Metropolitan Museum of Art. The girl becomes entranced with a statue that has baffled experts. She becomes determined to track down its former owner and uncover the secrets for herself. Based on the children's book From the Mixed-Up Files of Mrs Basil E. Frankweiler.

Inside Out (2015) Passes Bechdel
Set in the mind of a girl approaching puberty, it follows five personified emotions as they attempt to guide her through life. One the one hand it's a caper featuring cartoon blobs, on the other it contains important messages about mental health and growing up.

Nim's Island (2008) Passes Bechdel

Nim is a resourceful girl living on a remote island who is faced with a number of problems including a father who's gone missing, a neurotic children's author who isn't the hero she'd hoped and marauding Australian tourists.

Mary Poppins (1964) Passes Bechdel

Gotta love the IMDB summary of this: 'A magic nanny comes to work for a cold banker's unhappy family.' Well yes, but also a 1960s critique of patriarchy and capitalism. Mary Poppins is in control of everything and entirely independent. And it's got suffragettes.

Mulan (1998) Passes Bechdel

Disney's first attempt at a kickass female lead failed at the box office but the tale of a girl in old China who takes her father's place as a soldier and becomes a hero in the process has built up a following in the years since.

The Railway Children (1970) Not Bechdel listed

The Waterbury's happy middle-class Edwardian life is shattered when their father leaves one night without explanation. Their mother takes the children to the countryside where she earns money through writing. The children become fascinated with the railway line. I can break into tears just thinking about the ending. But that's not the point here. Bobby is clever and kind and spunky and it's a brilliant story about how children can be powerful in their own right.

The Rescuers (1974) Passes Bechdel

Two mice of the Rescue Aid Society search for a little girl kidnapped by unscrupulous treasure hunters. Though this shows its age now (there are some sexist comments that irritate me on every viewing in our house), it is unusual in having several main female characters of varying and interesting sorts – all of them are brave and forthright, including the baddie.

Labyrinth (1986) Passes Bechdel

Fifteen-year-old Sarah accidentally wishes her baby half-brother away to the Goblin King, Jareth, who will keep him if Sarah does not complete his labyrinth in 13 hours. Remember that important line, 'You have no power over me.' That's an important message for a teenage girl.

Kiki's Delivery Service (1989) Passes Bechdel

A young witch, on her mandatory year of independent life, finds fitting into a new community difficult while she supports herself by running an air courier service.

The Wild Thornberrys (2002) Not Bechdel listed

Eliza and Debbie are two sisters who don't always get along. But their relationship is put to the test when Debbie's life is in danger, and Eliza might have to give up her power to talk to animals.

Certificate PG (parental guidance)

Enchanted (2007) Passes Bechdel

An archetypal Disney Princess is dropped in the middle of modern-day New York. Soon after her arrival, Princess Giselle begins to change her views on life and love. Recommended by a follower because it's 'good at breaking stereotypes, challenges roles and she becomes self-employed!'

Castle in the Sky (1986) Not Bechdel listed

Inspired by *Gulliver's Travels*, the orphan Sheeta, with the help of Pazu and a rollicking band of sky pirates, makes her way to the ruins of the once great sky-kingdom of Laputa. Sheeta and Pazu must outwit the evil Muska.

Spirited Away (2001) Passes Bechdel

An Alice in Wonderland-style tale which sees Chihiro and her family wander into a world ruled by gods, witches and monsters. When her parents are changed into pigs Chihiro flees. She befriends a boy, and learns the rules of the land. Complex, layered and imaginative – not things often said about kids' films.

Nausicaä of the Valley of the Wind (1984) Not Bechdel listed

It's a thousand years since the war that almost wiped out the whole of the human race. A ship crashes in the valley and warrior/pacifist Princess Nausicaä desperately struggles to prevent two warring nations from destroying themselves and their dying planet. Described in one review as 'the only princess story worth watching'. She basically protects the whole planet.

MirrorMask (2005) Passes Bechdel

In a fantasy world of opposing kingdoms, a 15-year-old girl must find the fabled MirrorMask in order to save the kingdom and get home. This is not only a movie that passes the Bechdel test with flying colours, it's a film with a resourceful, intelligent and, most of all, believable young woman as a main character who overcomes long odds with her intellect and creativity.

Ever After: A Cinderella Story (1998) Passes Bechdel

The 'real' story of Cinderella. A refreshing take on the classic fairy tale – so says the blurb. Slightly sceptical about this one, but we haven't seen it, so feel free to tell us otherwise.

Brave (2012) Passes Bechdel

Determined to make her own path in life, Princess Merida defies a custom that brings chaos to her kingdom. Granted one wish, Merida must rely on her bravery and her archery skills to undo a beastly curse.

Bridge to Terabithia (2007) Passes Bechdel

A preteen's life is changed after befriending the new girl at school. We've already plot-spoiled this over on our book list, so we'll leave the summary at that. Haven't seen this film version but expect it to be thoughtful, sad and moving like the novel.

Whale Rider (2002) Passes Bechdel

A contemporary story of love, rejection and triumph as a young Maori girl fights to fulfil a destiny her grandfather refuses to recognise. A film that deals with the pain that a traditional patriarchal culture can bring into the life of a young girl. Powerful and beautiful.

Frozen (2013) Passes Bechdel

THE big Disney movie of recent years, we swithered over whether this qualified for this list. Although the marketing men have made it all about singing and Elsa's shimmery dress in the years since its release the film is still about two strong sisters who are brave, resourceful and independent. And upon its release that was a rarity.

Moana (2016) Passes Bechdel

Frozen proved to the execs that female-led movies could succeed, hence, three years later, this tale with a lead who is not just female but has brown skin! Moana sets out to prove herself a master wayfinder and along the way has to help a fallen demi-god. Also notable for a spirited older character in Moana's grandmother.

Zootropolis (2015) Passes Bechdel

Both the male and female leads in this animated caper about a city populated by animals have to overcome bullying and stereotyping about the roles they ought to play.

Alice in Wonderland (2010) Passes Bechdel

Tim Burton's rendering of the classic Lewis Carroll tale is predictably unpredictable but his Alice has agency. One parent tweeted us to say it was joyful hearing their daughter declare, 'I make the path!' Powerful and empowering stuff.

Certificate 12A (suitable for 12 years and over)

Ghostbusters (2016) Passes Bechdel

When it was announced that this remake of the 1984 classic would feature women playing the four lead roles taken by men in the original it certainly raised eyebrows. By doing so and succeeding it's hopefully triggered some different thinking in Hollywood. But best and most important of all the story of a quartet of oddballs teaming up to catch spooks in New York City still works as a knockout comedy movie.

Fast Girls (2012) Passes Bechdel

Shania and Lisa come from different backgrounds but both want to qualify for a major world athletics championship. The actresses trained alongside Team GB athletes to prepare for the roles. The film focuses on training hard to achieve a goal, which is nice. It's also funny, touching and action packed.

The Hunger Games (2012) Passes Bechdel

Sixteen-year-old Katniss Everdeen volunteers to take the place of her sister in the yearly Hunger Games where underprivileged youth fight to the death to entertain the rich and give hope to the poor – but not too much. In the ruins of North America she must go up against Tributes who have trained for the Games all their lives. Only one contestant can win.

Star Wars: The Force Awakens (2015) Passes Bechdel

We all left the cinema uplifted after this one. Not just because they had faithfully restored the Star Wars universe but best of all, the Jedi around which the saga looks set to revolve is a girl. (And her buddy Finn is less than the usual impervious, brave leading man – which is a good thing.) There's been few more gratifying sights in recent years than taking our young son to Star Wars-themed parties and seeing lots of little girls dressed as the impressive Rey.

NOTES

1. Bateson, Mary Catherine (German edition 1986, originally published 1984 in English) *With a Daughter's Eye: A Memoir of Margaret Mead and Gregory Bateson*. Hamburg: Rowohlt Verlag.

2. From an interview with Christiane Nüßlein-Volhard in Süddeutsche Zeitung.

3. Steinem, Gloria 'Our revolution has just begun.' Accessed on 26th May 2017 at msmagazine.com/blog/2015/03/21/our-revolution-has-just-begun

4. Grabrucker, Marianne (1981) *There's a Good Girl*, p.54.

5. Lowe, Pam, Your Letters, *Guardian*, 10th April 2017. Accessed on 16th April 2017 at/lifeandstyle/2010/apr/10/guardian-weekend-readers-letters

6. Fine, Cordelia (2011) *Delusions of Gender*. London: Icon Books Ltd, p.95.

7. Fine, Cordelia (2011) *Delusions of Gender*. London: Icon Books Ltd, p.96.

8. 'Life imitates art: Geena Davis on how gender inequality on TV and in movies has a powerful impact on kids.' *Wall Street Journal*, 11th April 2011.

9. 'Blue is for Boys.' *The F Word*, 9th November 2010. www.thefword.org.uk/2010/11/blue_is_for_boy

10. Fine, Cordelia (2011) *Delusions of Gender*. London: Icon Books Ltd, p.208.

11. 'Sex selection: Getting the baby you want.' *Guardian*, 3rd April 2010.

12. Lowe, Pam, Your Letters, *Guardian*, 10th April 2017. Accessed on 16th April 2017 at www.theguardian.com/lifeandstyle/2010/apr/10/guardian-weekend-readers-letters

13. Bloom, Lisa 'How to talk to little girls.' *Huffington Post*, 22nd June 2011.

14. 'A diet book for six-year-old girls: The worst idea ever?' *Guardian*, 17th August 2011.

15. 'A very sexist Christmas and a happy new year.' *The Crafty Bat*, 5th October 2011. Accessed on 14th March 2017 at http://thecraftybat. blogspot.co.uk/2011/10/very-sexist-christmas-and-happy-new.html

16. 'Feminism for early starters: Fairy tales and folk stories retold.' TreasuryIslands, 12th April 2011. Accessed on 16th April at https:// treasuryislands.wordpress.com/2011/02/28/feminism-picturebooks

17. 'Couple raise child as "gender neutral" to avoid stereotyping.' *Daily Telegraph*, 20th January 2012. Accessed on 14th March 2017 at www. telegraph.co.uk/news/9028479/Couple-raise-child-as-gender-neutral-to-avoid-stereotyping.html

18. Mott, Dr Helen 'Under-representation of females in pre-school children's television.' Accessed on 14th March 2017 at http://k003.kiwi6.com/ hotlink/7c4k4qw zvd/Nov08HMCBeebiesPresentation.pdf

19. 'Baby boy? Baby girl? Baby X!' *Neurotic Physiology*, 9th March 2011. Accessed on 14th March 2017 at http://scientopia.org/blogs/ scicurious/2011/03/09/baby-boy-baby-girl-baby-x

20. 'When did girls start wearing pink?' Smithsonian.com, 7th April 2011. Accessed on 14th March 2017 at www. smithsonianmag.com/arts-culture/when-did-girls-start-wearing-pink-1370097/?onsite_source=smithsonianmag.com&onsite_campaign=photogalleries&onsite_medium=internal&onsite_content=When+Did+Girls+Start+Wearing+Pink%3F

21. blue milk 'Adventures from the frontline: Running my first anti-sexism workshop with young children.' Hoyden About Town, 31st July 2011. Accessed on 14th March 2017 at https://bluemilk.wordpress. com/2011/07/31/adventures-from-the-frontline-running-my-first-anti-sexism-workshop-with-young-children

22. Tempel, Melissa Bollow 'One teacher's approach to preventing gender bullying in the classroom.' *Together for Jackson County Kids*, 16th December 2001. Accessed on 14th March 2017 at http:// togetherforjacksoncountykids.tumblr.com/post /14314184651/one-teachers-approach-to-preventing-gender

23. BBC News Online, 17th April 2012.

24. 'Will Sweden abolish the concept of gender?' iO9.com, 5th January 2012. Accessed on 15th April 2017 at http://io9.gizmodo.com/5906663/ will-sweden-abolish-the-concept-of-gender

25. Asher, Rebecca (2011) *Shattered: Modern Motherhood and the Illusion of Equality*. London: Harvill Secker.

26. 'Are dads the new moms?' *Wall Street Journal*, 11th May 2012.

27. Adam, Matthew, Walker, Carl and O'Connell, Paul (2001) 'Invisible or involved fathers? A content analysis of representations of parenting in young children's picture books.' *Sex Roles 65*, 3–4, 259–270.

28. 'How to talk to little girls.' *Huffington Post*, 22nd June 2011.

29. Slaughter, Anne-Marie 'Why women still can't have it all.' *Atlantic*, 13th June 2012. Accessed on 16th April at www.theatlantic.com/magazine/archive/2012/07/why-women-still-cant-have-it-all/309020/

30. 'Gender reading gap "not biological".' *London Evening Standard*, 2nd July 2012.

31. Hall, Celia 'Sexy high heels are worth the agony, say women.' *Daily Telegraph*, 3rd March 2001. Accessed on 16th April 2017 at http://www.telegraph.co.uk/news/uknews/1324862/Sexy-high-heels-are-worth-the-agony-say-women.html

32. *Think Progress*, 31st July 2012.

33. *Daily Telegraph*, 2nd August 2012 – the article now seems to have been taken down.

34. Schwyzer, Hugo 'Raising feminist sons: A conversation with Michael and Zachary Kimmel.' *RoleReboot*, 12th September 2012. Accessed on 17th April.

35. 'Abuse in Rochdale: Brutality meets a blind eye.' *Guardian*, 27th September 2012. Accessed on 13th March 2017 at www.theguardian.com/commentisfree/2012/sep/27/abuse-rochdale-brutality-blind-eye

36. Boone, Jon 'Pakistani girl shot over activism in Swat Valley, claims Taliban.' *Guardian*, 9th October 2012. Accessed on 13th March 2017 at www.theguardian.com/world/2012/oct/09/pakistan-girl-shot-activism-swat-taliban?CMP=twt_gu

37. 'Guess Who's sexist? Classic board game's gender bias leaves six-year-old fuming.' *Independent*, 17th November 2012.

38. O'Connell, Jennifer 'Update: response from Hasbro', 16th November 2012. Accessed on 13th March 2017 at www.byjenniferoconnell.com/2012/11/update-response-from-hasbro.html?m=1

39. Clifford, Stephanie 'More dads buy the toys, so Barbie, and stores, get makeovers.' *New York Times*, 3rd December 2012. Accessed on 17th April 2017 at www.nytimes.com/2012/12/04/business/more-dads-buy-the-toys-so-barbie-and-stores-get-makeovers.html

40. Villeroy and Boch 1264142091 4-Piece Play for Boys Children Cutlery Set, Amazon.co.uk. Accessed on 13th March 2017 at www.amazon.co.uk/Villeroy-Boch-1264142091-4-Piece-Children/dp/B0089C79GY/ref=sr_1_8?s=kitchen&ie=UTF8&qid=1356883059&sr=1-8

41. Paynter, Kelly Crisp 'Gender stereotypes and representation of female characters in children's picture books.' Liberty University, October 2011. Accessed on 13th March 2017 at http://digitalcommons.liberty.edu/doctoral/464

42. Hamilton, M., Anderson, D., Broaddus, M. and Young, K. (2006) 'Gender stereotyping and under-representation of female characters in 200 popular children's picture books: A twenty-first century update.' *Sex Roles 55*, 11–12, 757–765, p.764.

43. In Wade, Lisa 'Disney princesses, deconstructed.' *Sociological Images, The Society Pages*, 25th October 2009. Accessed on 13th March 2017 at http://thesocietypages.org/socimages/2009/10/25/disney-princesses-deconstructed

44. 'Research informs & empowers.' Geena Davis Institute on Gender in Media. Accessed on 16th April 2017 at https://seejane.org/research-informs-empowers

45. Women's Sport and Fitness Foundation (2012) *Changing the Game for Girls*. London: Women's Sport and Fitness Foundation. Accessed on 13th March 2017 at www.womeninsport.org/wp-content/uploads/2015/04/Changing-the-Game-for-Girls-Policy-Report.pdf

46. Brown, Andrew M. 'Women's judo: It's disturbing to watch these girls beat each other up.' *Daily Telegraph*, 2nd August 2012 – this article now seems to have been taken down.

47. Dunn, Carrie 'On the Olympics, sports in schools and new female role models.' *Bea Magazine*, 13th August 2012. Accessed on 13th March 2017 at https://beamagazine.wordpress.com/2012/08/13/on-the-olympics-sports-in-schools-and-new-female-role-models-by-carrie-dunn

48. Pablo Smith, Zoe 'Thanks (but no thanks…),' zoepablosmith, 23rd July 2012. Accessed on 13th March 2017 at https://zoepablosmith.wordpress.com/2012/07/23/thanks-but-no-thanks

49. www.change.org/p/stylist-fair-game-for-women-in-sport-campaign-fairgame

50. Skelton, Christine and Read, Barbara (2006) 'Male and female teachers' evaluative responses to gender and the implications of these for the learning environments of primary age pupils.' *International Studies in Sociology of Education 16*, 2, 105–120.

51. blue milk 'Adventures from the frontline: Running my first anti-sexism workshop with young children.' 31st July 2011. Accessed on 13th March 2017 at https://bluemilk.wordpress.com/2011/07/31/adventures-from-the-frontline-running-my-first-anti-sexism-workshop-with-young-children

52. Temple, Melissa Bollow '"It's okay to be neither": One teacher's approach to preventing gender bullying in a classroom.' *Together for Jackson County Kids*, 16th December 2011. Accessed on 13th March 2017 at http://togetherforjacksoncountykids.tumblr.com/post/14314184651/one-teachers-approach-to-preventing-gender

53. Note that this project has now come to an end and the website is no longer available.

54. Astell Project. Accessed on 16th April 2017 at http://www.astellproject.org.uk

55. Bengis, I. (1991) *Combat in the Erogenous Zone*. London: Harper Perennial, p.54.

56. Earp, Brian D. (2012) 'The extinction of masculine generics.' PhilPapers. Accessed on 15th April 2017 at https://philpapers.org/archive/EARTEO-3.pdf

57. Vintage British Argos 1976 Catalogue, Anthony Voz, Flickr, 28th December 2008. Accessed on 13th March 2017 at www.flickr.com/photos/38301877@N05/3589276287/in/set-72157619071382653

58. Swedish Institute (n.d.) *Gender Equality in Sweden.* Accessed on 13th March 2017 at https://sweden.se/society/gender-equality-in-sweden